Edison Romera

The idea of Latin America in the work of Darcy Ribeiro

Edison Romera

The idea of Latin America in the work of Darcy Ribeiro

An essay on Latin American social theory

ScienciaScripts

Imprint
Any brand names and product names mentioned in this book are subject to trademark, brand or patent protection and are trademarks or registered trademarks of their respective holders. The use of brand names, product names, common names, trade names, product descriptions etc. even without a particular marking in this work is in no way to be construed to mean that such names may be regarded as unrestricted in respect of trademark and brand protection legislation and could thus be used by anyone.

Cover image: www.ingimage.com

This book is a translation from the original published under ISBN 978-3-330-76417-0.

Publisher:
Sciencia Scripts
is a trademark of
Dodo Books Indian Ocean Ltd. and OmniScriptum S.R.L publishing group

120 High Road, East Finchley, London, N2 9ED, United Kingdom
Str. Armeneasca 28/1, office 1, Chisinau MD-2012, Republic of Moldova, Europe
Managing Directors: Ieva Konstantinova, Victoria Ursu
info@omniscriptum.com

Printed at: see last page
ISBN: 978-620-8-09283-2

ACKNOWLEDGMENTS

I am completely and immensely grateful to my mother Vera Lucia and my sister Carolina Romera. Their good-natured support, words of encouragement, pertinent advice and, above all, the love they always offered me unconditionally, made me persevere in the face of difficulties.

Carolina Diniz Abreu, the beautiful woman I met and who, together, we decided to share our lives with, has made me happy and full of hope for a better future. The care, affection and affection you have shown me have been essential to reassure me and keep me focused, without which this work would be penalized. I love you every day!

My greatest thanks go to my advisor, Dr.ª Adelia Maria Miglievich-Ribeiro. For the many productive conversations and for readily accepting me as a student advisor, setting challenges and being patient with my limitations, she encouraged me to be better than I thought I could be. The support he gave me - even when far away - both institutional and academic, as well as personal and human, through his guidance and corrections, dedication and sensitivity, were what made this work possible. On this journey, as well as proving to be a brilliant teacher and a reliable reference in whom I look up to, she has also become a good and dear friend. Any merit this work may receive must also be credited to her.

Far from undervaluing the importance of all the other professors who took part in my undergraduate education, I would like to give special thanks to Dr. Marta Zorzal e Silva, who kindly provided all the necessary academic support that resulted in the completion of this work; and also to Dr. Sonia Missagia de Mattos; and to PhD student Claudio Marcio Coelho who, at various times, offered me remarkable affection and special attention, to which I will always remain tenderly indebted.

As for the friends who have worked with me and are still working towards reflection and *praxis,* in other words, the conscious and transformative action of a sociology that makes sense of our reality, you know that there are many names to thank. It is true that many come to mind and I sincerely wish to salute them all. However, I would like to point out that, for fear of some name being forgotten, not on purpose, but due to an occasional oversight, I prefer to attribute my affection to all those who have surrounded me and lived with me, and still do. Because each and every one of them knows how important and valuable they are.

Last but not least, to the Triune God, the highest praise and gratitude. "For from him and through him and to him are all things. To him be glory for ever. Amen!".

SUMMARY

PREFACE

"Unity is what we lack" (Leopoldo Zea)

This work recovers Darcy Ribeiro's trajectory as an intellectual who focused primarily on Latin American issues. The author focuses on studies by Mignolo (2003), Miglievich-Ribeiro (2012, 2013), Coelho (2012), Bomeny (2011), and Vaz e Silva (2009).

As a contribution, he gives us an in-depth look at Darcy's Studies in the Anthropology of Civilization, highlighting his role as an interlocutor in our research and dialogues with the social and political reality of Latin America.

Throughout this book, we come across the influences and networks of sociability that founded the thinker Darcy Ribeiro, inspiring his countless achievements. Among them, we highlight Simon Bolivar and Jose Marti, and in Brazil, Manoel Bomfim and Gilberto Freyre. On the other hand, in another of Darcy's texts, *Configurates Historico-Culturais dos Povos Americanos,* the study contributes to the deepening of analysis on the subject, which certainly adds to other dialogues and reflections on the contribution of Darcy Ribeiro's work towards a better understanding of what Brazilian identity is. It also helps us to investigate the paths and vicissitudes of the formation of Latin America up to the present day.

In the first chapter, Edison Romera points out the cultural historical process that runs through the roots and open veins of Latin America, contributing to possible and multiple identities. The author highlights how the question of identity runs through the foundations of nationality in each of the different countries that make up the continent.

Based on Bolivar's question, *"Que somos nosotros los pueblos americanos, entre los pueblos, las civilizaciones",* Ribeiro (1943) analyzes the philosophical, historical and cultural dimensions that permeate Bolivar's thinking.
At the same time, he always dialogued with Leopoldo Zea, an important intellectual who was part of the Darcynian networks of sociability.

For many intellectuals, and particularly for Darcy, Bolivar would have been a "Don Quixote of America", perhaps the true thinker of the project of a single, Latin

American Patria. For Darcy, the *Patria Grande* (1986).

It is also worth highlighting in Bolivar's thinking the republican bases for the future political organization of our American states, which can also be seen throughout Darcyn's thinking, the defense of the consolidation of republican institutions.

Another character also featured in this book is the Cuban Jose Marti, considered one of the most important intellectuals in Latin America for his political stance.

The dream of the Patria Grande, so cherished by Darcy Ribeiro, originates in the dreams of Jose Marti, back in the 19th century, in his best-known text, *Nuestra America*. For the Cuban poet, we had a "peculiar American soul".

In this sense, what the study points to when analyzing Darcy Ribeiro's thinking is the strong imprint of Bolivar's and Marti's ideals on future Darcynian writings. It is worth highlighting his great contribution, among others, to the theoretical field of Anthropology, particularly in relation to Latin America.

The author of this book set out to investigate Darcy Ribeiro as a thinker on Latin American issues. And already at the end of the first chapter, we can say that he has succeeded in his initial aims. The work that I preface was the result of his monograph at the end of his degree course in Social Sciences at the Federal University of Espirito Santo, supervised by researcher Adelia Miglievich-Ribeiro, a scholar of anthropologist Darcy Ribeiro. On the other hand, I was fortunate enough to supervise her post-doctoral research at PROPED/UERJ on Darcy Ribeiro's legacy during his years in exile at a Latin American university, specifically in Peru.

Therefore, when I visit the writings of Edison Romera, I also revisit the contributions of this young UFES researcher, Professor Adelia. In this way, I realize the formation of a network of sociability, which has been growing stronger among PROPED/UFES, and through productions on Darcy Ribeiro.

At this point, I would also like to point out young researchers who have been contributing to the field.

These are Leonardo Nolasco, in his post-doctorate (PROPED|UERJ); Vittorio lo Bianco (PhD/PPIT/UERJ), and Silvio Souza (PhD/PPFIT/UERJ), among others. These studies have been carried out by the Laboratorio Educagao e Republica (LER/PROPED/UERJ), of which Adelia is an associate professor.

The second chapter explores Darcy's dialogues with the works of Gilberto

Freyre and Manoel Bonfim, two Northeastern thinkers for whom Darcy had great respect and admiration. Although he kept a critical eye on their writings.

For Ribeiro, *Casa Grande e Senzala* was the most important work of Brazilian culture. On the other hand, his greatest criticism was directed at researchers in the fields of History, Social Sciences and Philosophy who had never met Manoel Bomfim, as well as anthropologists who didn't read and even despised Gilberto Freyre, Arthur Ramos or Josue de Castro.

Romera successfully deepens his investigation into the interlocution between the thinking of the three intellectuals - Ribeiro, Freire and Bonfim - once again anchoring himself theoretically in the studies of Miglievich-Ribeiro (2013) and Coelho (2000).

What can be observed throughout this work is that Darcy is being constructed in his different skins and ways. Not just as an anthropologist, but also as a writer and novelist, in a dialogue between theoretical writings and literature, as in his first novel, *Maira* (1976), which reveals his view of the Indians from themselves and that of civilized whites.

Finally, in chapter three, the author sets out to analyze the Darcynian interpretation of Latin America even further. He begins by investigating the exile as an initial milestone after the military coup on March 31, 1964.

Darcy's choice of Latin America, starting with Uruguay, allowed him to expand and strengthen his network of sociability with intellectuals from that continent, such as Eduardo Galeano. A significant moment was his appointment as president of the "Seminar for the Reform of the University of Uruguay". From this experience, his book *The Necessary University was* born.

Also in Uruguay, he completed *The Civilizing Process* and *The Indians and Civilization.*

During his 12 years in exile, as Romera points out, his output was astonishing.

In his final chapter, the author emphasizes the centrality of two concepts proposed by Darcy. The categories of "historical updating" and "evolutionary acceleration". In this way, he highlights how Darcy sought elements for a better understanding of the Latin American reality, starting from the cultural level, countering the situation of dependence in relation to the political centers of power.

In an original way, Darcy developed an explanatory theory for the formation and founding of Latin America. He called this classification *Historical-Cultural*

Configurations, which were national ethical typologies called: Witness-Peoples; New-Peoples; Transplanted-Peoples and Emerging-Peoples.

The one that occupies the most space in his reflections refers to the New Peoples, which includes Brazil (Mattos, 2007). This historical and cultural configuration originates from the "combination, deculturization and melding of disparate ethnic matrices such as the indigenous, African and European". For Ribeiro, they constitute the most representative configuration of the Americas, since they permeate the entire continent, including Brazil, Paraguay, Venezuela, Colombia, Chile and the Antilles, part of Central America and the South of the United States (Ribeiro, 1975).

Finally, Romera closes this third chapter by once again highlighting the issue of Latin American identity. At this point, among other aspects, he points to the linguistic-cultural level, recalling the Luso-American content found in Brazil, while the American content characterizes the rest of the continent (Ribeiro, 1986).

Therefore, throughout the book, what stands out in Darcyn's thinking is the strength of the UTOPIA of a single, Latin American nation. Latin America has always existed under the sign of utopia. I'm even convinced that utopia has its place and place here (Ribeiro, 1986, p.65).

At the end of this preface, which I had the pleasure of writing, I am certain that we are already a tribe of scholars and academics who have recognized the revolutionary potential of the thought and deeds of this valued Brazilian, Darcy Ribeiro.

Congratulations Edison, I'll end by echoing your words:

"In other words, we have chosen Darcy Ribeiro as one of the authors of greatest significance and relevance for the understanding and socio-cultural interpretation of the American peoples."

Lia Faria Fazenda Boa Sorte, T rajano de Moraes, July 14, 2017

INTRODUCTION

Darcy Ribeiro was an intellectual-militant and polymath thinker. He performed a wide variety of roles and tasks as an anthropologist, educator, politician, writer, essayist and novelist, teacher and *utopian*, since he dedicated himself to studying Latin America and, in particular, Brazil, which could and should work. He was a public figure who achieved international prominence and recognition, although his work and legacy were sparsely disseminated by the national *intelligentsia*. In short, he is not a personality that can be grasped without recognizing all his complexity.

Agnaldo dos Santos and Isa G. Ferraz (2014, p. 325) say that he was "a man of a thousand faces. Brilliant, restless, funny, provocative, polemical, he was a volcano in permanent ebullition". However, overemphasizing his supposed *exceptionality* could easily lead to some misunderstandings. Darcy Ribeiro publicly criticized his peers, particularly academics. Upon his return from exile and engagement in political activities in the early 1980s, the acidity of his criticism of a type of academic production and his re-immersion in public life contributed significantly to the caricatured image of him as an intellectual antagonistic to any kind of "academicism", which became inseparable from his own personality (MATTOS, 2007). But caution is advised when accepting such an iconoclastic image, even though his strong opinions appealed to what he thought was most salutary and urgent, the resumption of an authentic *anthropology of civilization.*

Darcy was born on October 26, 1922, in the city of Montes Claros, in the northern region of Minas Gerais. He died in 1997, at the age of 74, respected as a brilliant intellectual by countless voices, never consensual, given the ideological battles that underlay his writings. A "man of faith and of party" (RIBEIRO, 1997), his thought and work were aligned with the ideals of a solidary and emancipatory society that creatively went back to some classics to motivate developments through interesting debates and theoretical reconstructions of the most stimulating kind[1] .

Strictly speaking, the guiding question of this essay was the perception of the idea of Latin America in the work of Darcy Ribeiro, more specifically in the writings he called *Estudos de Antropologia da Civilizaçao* (*Studies in the Anthropology of Civilization),* produced over 30 years of vigorous intellectual life.

---

[1] As an example of this understanding of Darcy Ribeiro's work, we cite works by Walter D. Mignolo (2003), Adelia Miglievich-Ribeiro (2011[2] ; 2013), Haydee

In the book *Latinoamericanos a procura de um lugar neste seculo,* by the Argentine anthropologist Nestor Garcia Canclini[2] , the author opens his first pages by stating that "it is not simple today to speak of Latin America as a whole" (CANCLINI, 2008, p. 11), which serves as a warning about the still present and pertinent discussion about the concept and meanings surrounding this nomenclature, as well as the economic, political and cultural issues that permeate the continent in question. Seeing Darcy Ribeiro as a prominent interlocutor in this dispute, we have chosen his work and theories with an eye to their possible resonances in today's Latin American integration proposals, with greater or lesser ambiguity in terms of affecting world geopolitics.

Darcy Ribeiro, in his attempt to make sense of Latin America's reality, does not start exclusively from a detailed personal observation. Without fear, he declares that he is indebted to other theorists, or like him, *intellectuals-militants*, who have already set out before him to understand Latin America and make it one of the "most progressive, just and prosperous continental expressions on earth" (RIBEIRO, 1995, p. 204). The first chapter of our monograph recalls this influence, particularly Simon Bolivar and Jose Marti, as key figures in Darcyn's intellectual and ideological journey. The second chapter continues in this vein, but looks at sources closer to Darcy Ribeiro, in particular, two outstanding Northeasterners: Manoel Bomfim and Gilberto Freyre, on whom Darcy Ribeiro produced beautiful and copiously praised essays, as we shall see below. The latter also exerted a significant influence, each in their own way, guiding the positions, emphases and discussions worked on by the anthropologist from Minas Gerais.

In a third moment, we turn our attention in more detail to the theme of Latin America within the scope of Darcyn's work. We try to outline, within the space available, the inseparable importance of his experiences, *achievements* and "walks" through the Spanish-American countries, with the break from a "provincial" posture, to assume a greater honor, that of a *Latin-American citizen.*

As a result, we will deal with their theoretical and explanatory innovation regarding the backwardness of this colonized and dispossessed people. The reasons for what they are and what they can be. As well as specifying, within the *Historical-*

[2] In this work, Canclini (2008) tried to outline a contemporary diagnosis of the possibilities, potentialities and obstacles to Latin American integration, presenting proposals to carry out tasks that, in his opinion, are possible and feasible, especially in the socio-cultural field; with the aim of demonstrating how Latin America can foster a competitive economy in the context of globalization.

Cultural Configurations elaborated by Darcy, the constitution of the whole of Latin America as a continental civilization deserving of all respect from the other parts of humanity.

CHAPTER I - FORMATION AND IMPORTANCE

1.1 Emancipation

It is possible to say that the formation of Latin American thought is the history of the idea of Latin America itself, being the formation of an idea that develops, organizes, breaks and recreates realities in its own historical dynamics. Some issues have been of significant importance, such as its identity and, based on this, its integration to the detriment and distinction from colonial impositions since 1492 (ZEA, 1993). As Leopoldo Zea pointed out, "unity is what we lack" (*apud* TRETO, 1996, p.43).

It would be no exaggeration to say that the fundamental theme of Latin American thought is the national question, both existing and projected. This is what Octavio Lanni suggests when he points out that, "the history of Latin America can be seen as that of the Latin American nation, in the sense of its formation and consolidation" (IANNI, 1993, p. 32).

Such concerns preceded the political emancipation movements in America. From the first wars and independence revolutions at the beginning of the 19th century to the controversies over authoritarianism and democracy, or capitalism and socialism, at the end of the 20th century, many, if not most, have dealt with national issues.

> From the caudillesque stumbles in the provinces, at the beginning of the formation of the national state, to the popular revolutions that have multiplied in this century, many have dealt with the way in which the nation is formed. This is Bolivar's theme (...). From various perspectives, Latin American social thought and history are crossed by the national question.
>
> The national question concerns how the nation is formed and transformed. It begins by establishing that the nation is not an articulated whole, ready, finished. On the contrary, it finds that it is a whole in movement, in process, in becoming. Not only is it formed and transformed it is also articulated and disaggregated (IANNI, 1993, p. 33).

The question of identity, which is intertwined with the national question, has been a practical and theoretical dilemma since the dawn of history. This dilemma is summed up primarily and precisely in the wars and revolutions of independence. For what we can characterize as epic in the struggles waged and symbolized by Simon

Bolivar, for example, among many others, is rooted in the quest to emancipate the colony, form the state, organize the nation by removing it from colonialism, absolutism and mercantilism, and giving it a name, an identity.

Darcy Ribeiro proposes a reflection on the aspiration of what history has called the *Liberator* - *a* title given to Bolivar for whom "he had embodied the will to be free of a continent and who had strived to create a political world of justice and human rights" (PIETRI, 1992, p. 62). In a rich ontology of Latin American philosophical and historical-cultural dimensions, compiled by Leopoldo Zea, there is an essay by Darcy Ribeiro under the title, *La Cultura Latinoamericana,* in which he states, "Bolivar's question continues to resonate. ^What are we, the American people, among the people, the civilizations?" (RIBEIRO, 1993, p. 101). Ribeiro goes on to explain his arguments on the premise that much has already been written on the subject in question - which Latin America? - However, the more often fragmentary stories, circumstantial observations and, above all, anecdotal "causos" are disseminated[3] .

Darcyn's initial choice of Bolivar is emblematic, as he is considered to be one of the most important figures for the freedom and autonomy of the Latin American peoples. In him we saw action and avant-garde thinking like few others, or even, it would be "pointless to try to draw parallels" as Silvio Julio (1957, p. 139) points out. It is common to read a variety of praises; for example, Castelar, who had been president of the Spanish ministry, declared: "The conquest of American freedom is

---

[3] Despite the salutary Darcynian criticism, it is possible to describe among the most important works of Latin American intellectual production, their mentions in a punctual way, which according to Ianni, can give an idea of the repeated challenge that this problematic exerts: "In Argentina: Domingo F. Sarmiento, *Facundo* (Civilizacion y Barbarie); Juan B. Alberdi, *Bases y Puntos de Partida para la Organization Politico de la Republica Argentina;* Ezequiel Martinez Estrada, *Radiografia de la Pampa;* Jose Hernandez, *Martin Fierro.* In Peru: Jose Carlos Mariategui, *Siete Ensayos* de *Interpretation de la Realidad Peruana;* Victor Raul Haya de la Torre, *El Imperialismo y el Apra;* Jose Maria Arguedas, *Todas las Sangres;* Julio Cotler, *Estado y Nation en el Peru.* In Mexico: Andres Molina Enriquez, *Los Grandes Problemas Nacionales;* Samuel Ramos, *El Perfil del Hombre y la Cultura en Mexico;* Octavio Paz, *El Laberinto de la Soledad;* Pablo Gonzalez Casanova, *La Democracia en Mexico;* as well as Mexican muralist painting by Orozco, Rivera and Siqueiros. In Puerto Rico: Antonio S. Pedreira, *Insularismo;* Tomas Blanco, *Prontuario Historico de Puerto Rico;* Manuel Maldonado Denis, *Puerto Rico: una Interpretation Historico-Social;* Jose Luis Gonzalez, *El Pais de Cuatro Pisos;* Angel G. Quintero Rivera, *Clases Sociales e Identidad National*, Luis Pales Matos, *Tuntun de Pasa y Grifena;* Manuel A. Alonso, *El Gibaro.* In Brazil: Oliveira Vianna, *Evolugao do Povo Brasileiro;* Gilberto Freyre, *Interpretação do Brasil;* Sergio Buarque de Holanda, *Raizes do Brasil;* Caio Prado Junior, *Evolugao Polftica do Brasil;* Jose Honorio Rodrigues, *Aspiragoes Nacionais;* Raymundo Faoro, *Os Donos do Poder;* Florestan Fernandes, *A Revolugao Burguesa no Brasil;* Lima Barreto, *Triste Fim de Policarpo Quaresma;* Mario de Andrade, *Macunaima.* All of them are interested in understanding how people, society, the state and the nation are formed; at certain junctures or throughout history. There are dilemmas relating to social, cultural, racial, regional and other diversities. They rescue and forget real and imagined traditions, while at the same time narrating controversies and struggles, fantasies and utopias." (IANNI, 1993, p. 74, emphasis added).

the greatest achievement of the century. The greatest achievement, worthy of a great artist. And Bolivar was an artist" *(apud* DIETRICH, 1937, p. 231). Or even his enemies, as in the case of his greatest adversary, General Morillo, who wrote of him: "His heroism and his virtues are a guarantee that he will remain at the head of the revolution and the liberating army: he is the Revolution" *(apud* DIETRICH, 1937, p. 231). Even the famous Spanish philosopher Miguel de Unamuno also said that Bolivar was a true and complete man, and this, according to Unamuno, means being more than a "superman", in his words, it means that, "he was one of the greatest heroes in whom the Spanish soul was personified, the spiritual element without which humanity would be incomplete" *(apud* DIETRICH, 1937, p. 231). In other words, Unamuno, through a discourse of appropriation, adapted and nationalized the figure of Bolivar to a diffuse Hispanidad, making him, to a certain extent, the glory of his land and his people. Bolivar's admiration led him to identify him as a Spanish man, and even more so as a liberated "Don Quijote of Hispanic America". Unamuno elevated him to the hero of humanity.

It is possible to perceive a certain enthusiasm and excessive praise in these descriptions. However, what interests us here is that Simon Bolivar, at the time of independence, envisioned a confederation of Spanish-American republics, with the aim of forming a "single nation". He was "the greatest creator and defender of a unifying political project for Hispanic America" (DORATIOTO, 1994, p. 33). And already in his first phase of seeking independence, he suffered a defeat, which forced him to seek asylum on an English island, and in 1815, he proposed a confederative project from that same island, which became known as the "Charter of Jamaica", in which he stated:

> I wish more than anyone else to see the greatest nation in the world formed in America, less for its extension and riches than for its freedom and glory. Although I aspire to the perfection of my country's government, I cannot persuade myself that the New World will be governed by a great republic for the time being. (...) It is a grandiose idea to intend to form a single nation out of the entire New World, with a single link connecting its parts to each other and to the whole. Since it has one origin, one language, one customs and one religion, it should therefore have a single government that would confederate the different states that might be formed; but this is not possible, because remote climates, different situations, opposing interests, different characters, divide America. How beautiful it would be if the isthmus of Panama were for us what the isthmus of Corinth was for the Greeks! (...) Surely union is what we need to complete the work of our regeneration. However, our division is not strange, because this is the distinguishing feature of civil wars, which are generally between two parties: *conservatives and reformers.* (...) Yo dire a Vd. what can put us in a position to expel the

> Spaniards and found a free government: *union,* certainly; but this union will not sell us by divine prodigies but by sensible effects and well-directed efforts (BOLIVAR, 1993, p. 27 *et seq.* emphasis added).

This letter was enough to paint a significant and audacious picture of his vision of American destiny, and it was there that his fundamental conception was set: the imperial structure of colonial rulers could not continue. Throughout the independence process, the task of organizing the power that Bolivar embodied became essential (SARMIENTO, 1993). However, it was not simply a question of Latin American liberation from the metropole, but of recreating institutions on a republican basis. Until then, the administrative structures and ideologies had been imported, under the conditions in which the colonial enterprise had been organized, so that the administration was riddled with such remnants, and "[there was] therefore a need to create something new" (BELLOTTO and CORREA, 1983, p. 20). Bolivar, with each conquest, did not limit himself to replacing the old administrative body; he went further, committing himself to extinguishing the colonial institutions and establishing a new administration, based on the principles of liberalism and adapted to the American reality and context. It is clear that the question of political organization is present in his writings, both in his "defence of liberal principles" and in his reference to "the real possibilities of organizing and maintaining a state that was born under a heavy burden of commitments" (BELLOTTO and CORREA, 1983, p. 21).

Bolivar's proposal for the political organization of the new American states can be found in his speech to the Venezuelan Congress in Angostura - dated February 15, 1819 - where he set out his concept of national sovereignty and, at the same time, presented a draft constitution, which was considered an essential document in his political ideology (BELLOTTO and CORREA, 1983, p. 22). This document defends the need to start from reality itself, the reality experienced by women and men in America. This led *el Libertador* towards questions concerning the identity of those who were freed. A complex identity, which needed to be clarified in order to understand and know what they are, what they want and also what they can achieve. His proposal was not to imitate, without repeating, but to recreate, otherwise they would be caught up in a new dependency (BOLIVAR, 1993[2]). Bolivar, in his time, anticipated the analysis of the issues that challenge the future of Latin America.

At the end, we can say in summary that,

> Bolivar envisioned the formation of a great American nation, organized along liberal lines. However, for Bolivar, the possession of power was accompanied by disappointments. The initial image of a great liberal nation gradually drifted away from the original project. Bolivar, in his obstinacy to remain in charge, not admitting competitors or not having the ability to share power with his comrades, remained faithful to the ideal formulated in his youth until his last moment, even though struck down by the difficulties posed by a state in the process of being organized, feeling prematurely aged, wounded by the hidden enemy of illness and pain. Having faced countless battles, in the open or in political debates, he ended up being defeated, beaten by the disappointments of broken dreams and by the illness that made him prematurely old at the age of 47 (BELLOTTO and CORREA, 1983, p. 22).

1.2 Our America

In a way, arms and letters, politics and poetic writing concomitantly founded the new American profile, outlining the characteristics of this autochthonous subject. Like Simon Bolivar, we find another character who stimulated and fought for Latin American utopia, the Cuban Jose Marti (18531895). Considered one of the most important intellectuals in Latin America, he was responsible for the production of more than 1,500 texts, including fiction, poetry, chronicles, letters and, above all, for maintaining a unique political position throughout his life, and a public intellectual stance, seeking to inaugurate a new discursive *ethos* in relation to Latin American history, culture and identity. He "refuses to understand the history of Latin America from the point of view of the colonizer and the landmark of the conquest, that is, the arrival of the European on American soil" (VELOSO, 2011, p. 134).

Bolivar is also credited with having a significant influence on Marti's thinking, the latter being considered his continuator[4] Pedro Rodriguez (2006) points out that the importance Marti gave Bolivar was based on the latter's ideas about continental unity, a hot topic in Latin American historiography.

Historically, what is known as Latin America has been, and to a certain extent continues to be, a tumultuous and mutinous scenario in which ideas and projects

[4] "Before settling permanently in New York, Marti spent several months in Venezuela, where he developed some of the Bolivarian ideals that would become part of his internationalist philosophy. (...) He also evoked Bolivar 's internationalist dream , arguing in favor of 'a great confederation of Latin American peoples'. " GOTT, 2006, p. 1.) He also evoked Bolivar's internationalist dream, arguing in favor of 'a great confederation of the peoples of Latin America'." GOTT, 2006, p. 105. Cf. also: SADER, 1985, p. 9; PUENTES e NAVIA, 2004, p. 49; BRUCE, 2012, p. 1; VELOSO, 2011, p. 136. Also noteworthy is a text by Marti himself (1993[2]), entitled *Simon Bolivar,* in homage to the *liberator.*

formulated by leaders and intellectuals who, each operating in their own way and based on different approaches and references, seek to vindicate and impose a field of autochthonous identity, clash. Especially in the post-independence period, marked by a specific socio-historical configuration of strong identity conflict and continuous struggles to define the means necessary for nation-building. Among the identity proposals and possibilities on offer, especially in 19th century Hispano-America, the dream of a "Patria Grande" (Great Homeland)[5] deserves special mention, as it gained greater solidity in the inseparable work and life of Jose Marti, in particular and from his best-known text, *Nuestra America,* of which not only Hispanic America but also Brazil[6] are part, and "towards which we are still moving in the direction of greater cultural, political, economic, academic and philosophical integration" (BRUCE, 2012, p. 1). 1). This text has become profoundly significant, since, according to Boaventura de S. Santos, it is possible to see that, "Marti expresses (...) a series of ideas that others - such as Mariategui and Oswald de Andrad, Fernando Ortiz and Darcy Ribeiro - have continued" (SANTOS, 2004).

Nuestra America was an effort to interpret Latin America from within Latin America itself. In other words, it does not fail to recognize the influence of the West on our culture and history, but gives significant importance to understanding us from our specificities. For Rodriguez (2006), the entire work and life of the Cuban thinker is based on two essential axes: his Latin Americanism and his anti-imperialism. Thus, it was not without reason that, in 1875, while in exile in Mexico, Marti used the expression "our America" for the first time, writing: "If Europe were the brain, our

[5] This theme and concept also served as an inspiration - keeping in mind the proportions of use, focus, objectives and theorization - for the reflections produced by Darcy Ribeiro, expressed in a significant way in a collection of essays entitled: *Latin America: A Patria Grande.* It was originally published in 1986 with the intention of revisiting the theme of Latin American identity from a historical, cultural, political and social perspective. Subsequently, two of the essays that make up the book - "Does Latin America exist?" and "Latin American political typology" - were published in *Cadernos do Parlatino* (BRITO, Jose D. (org.) *Cadernos do Parlatino*, n° 13, Sao Paulo, Latin American Parliament, January 1998), edited by the Latin American Parliament of Sao Paulo, bringing together a collection of texts by Darcy Ribeiro organized by Jose Domingos de Brito. The Latin American Parliament's tribute with this publication can be reciprocated with the words of Darcy Ribeiro himself: "The best thing, however, was a São Paulo invention that I didn't take part in. The building of the headquarters of the Latin American Parliament inside the memorial (Memorial da América Latina) (...) The Latin American Parliament will have the same function of structuring the future Latin American nation dreamt of by Bolivar. Our cultural, linguistic and even ethnic identity is much deeper, which will make Sao Paulo and the memorial, tomorrow, the capital of the Latin American nation" (RIBEIRO, 1997, p. 482.).

[6] The theme of Portuguese America in contrast to Hispanic America, due to its formation and maintenance of the Empire and black slavery when, at the time of independence, the Spanish colonized nations repudiated such institutions, The delicate insertion of Brazil into the Latin American project will be considered here at the right time, while we will notice in Darcy Ribeiro a tireless commitment to the integration of Brazil into its own continent, something rejected, for example, by Simon Bolivar.

America would be the heart" *(apud* RODRIGUEZ, 2006, p. 39). In short, it can be exemplified in the following way, that for Marti:

- Latin America is made up of new peoples.

- There is a particular American nature there, that is to say, spiritual characteristics, social psychology, that are proper and peculiar.

- The particularities and specificities of the US require their own analysis and solutions: "For specific conflicts, specific solutions" (apud RODRIGUEZ, 2006, p. 11).

Marti was able to progressively mature his concept of continental unity, as well as the construction of a Latin American identity. He proposed a path towards Cuban national liberation and a sensible integration of the continent, together with a healthy critique of liberalism, republicanism, positivism and certain ideas of technical and scientific progress held by Latin American intellectuals and politicians.

Eugenio Carvalho (1998) argues that through the concept of *Nuestra America,* Marti sought to delineate his own identity dimension and perspective. This concept goes beyond geographical, political, linguistic and ethnic boundaries. For the Cuban poet, along with historical and cultural elements, the basis of an identity lies in the idea of a peculiar *American soul*. In other words, this "spirit" or "continental soul" is based on the synthesis of a pre-established set of values, purposes and interests shaped by an ethical model created by Marti[7] . This can be poetically perceived in the following Martinian elocution:

> To those who, with less favor from History, are climbing the path of republics

[7] It is worth mentioning here, although it is long but necessary, the warning that "many authors who focus on this aspect in Martiana's work sometimes fail to realize how many proposals for unity and identity are marked by the emotions and professions of faith of their enunciators, almost always unrelated to a corresponding desire or feeling of identity on the part of those they represent. 'Los pueblos castellanos de America han de volverse a juntar pronto, donde se vera, o donde se vera. El corazon se lo pide'. (...) The unity of integration at continental level can be understood as a practical requirement, but unlike the older national units, it is not associated with intense feelings. The consequence of this is that the statement 'I am Latin American', for example, is emotionally weak. It remains to be seen to what extent, considering Marti's time, the individuals who lived in the countless tribes, slave quarters, fields, mountains and cities of 'Nuestra America', regardless of their ethnic and/or national ties, actually felt 'Latin American'. Taking this component into account is fundamental to better understanding and measuring the process of constituting identities" (CARVALHO, 1998, p. 77).

> to heroic heights; nor can they hide the evident facts of the problem that can be solved, for the peace of the centuries, with the opportune study and the tacit and urgent union of the continental soul. Because the unanimous dream is already over; the current generation is leading the working America to the hills, along the path paved by the sublime fathers; from Bravo to Magallanes, sitting on the condor's back, the Great Semi rules, through the romantic nations of the continent and through the painful isles of the sea, the seed of the new America! (MARTI, 1993, p. 127).

Marti thus proposed a form of understanding and experience of autochthonous Latin America, thus creating "a new people, different from the Aboriginals and the Spanish" (RODRIGUEZ, 2006, p.12); characterized by a mestigagem, more specifically in its configuration and architecture, that is, referring to culture rather than the biological aspect. This concept can be exemplified later in the words of the Brazilian poet Oswald de Andrade (1990), when he published *A Utopia Antropofagica.* Anthropophagy is metaphorically understood as the ability to assimilate, or even *anabolize, a* critical process of cultural formation. This cannibalistic perspective, here positive and innovative, would allow for the critical appropriation of foreign ideas in the sphere of culture. The anthropophagist, in this case, would be able to swallow imported forms or conceptions in order to develop a genuinely autonomous identity profile:

> I'm only interested in what's not mine. Man's law. Law of the anthropophagist. (...) Against all importers of canned consciousness. The tangible existence of life. This is the pre-logical mentality for Mr. Levy-Bruhl to study. (...) I asked a man what law was. He told me that it was the guarantee of the exercise of possibility. The man's name was Galli Mathias. (...) Anthropophagy. Absorption of the sacred enemy. To turn him into a totem. The human adventure. The earthly goal. However, only the pure elites have succeeded in carrying out carnal anthropophagy, which brings with it the highest meaning of life and avoids all the evils identified by Freud, catechist evils (ANDRADE, 1990, p. 47-51).

In line with Martin's mestipagem, it is possible to cite the anthropologist Darcy Ribeiro, who expresses himself without any embarrassment, imbued with a strong provocative humor, and who, despite being long, is a quote that absolutely exemplifies the anthropophagy of every Brazilian:

> It's very easy to make an Australia: take half a dozen French, English, Irish and Italians, throw them on a desert island, they kill the Indians and make a fucking second-rate England, or a third-rate one, that shit.
> Brazil needs to learn that it is shit, that Canada is shit, because it repeats Europe. And to see that we have the adventure of making the human race new, the mestipagem in the flesh and in the spirit. Mestipo is good.
> My flesh in Europe was never taken for Portuguese, Spanish or Greek. They

> asked if I was Persian, because I looked much more like an Arab, who looks much more like an Indian.
> These old faces of ours are not viable in Europe. So we made a people capable of inheriting 10,000 years of indigenous wisdom, of adapting to the tropics and making a tropical civilization. Then the Europeans arrived here, planting wheat. These people are there and I say that we are the new Rome. In Rome, they want me to go and talk about it, they want me to write more articles. And why the new Rome? We're the biggest Latin mass. The French are jerking off, the Italians are drinking chianti, the Romanians are afraid of the Russians, the Spanish and Portuguese are fucking around and we've made a mass of people that is 500 million (RIBEIRO, 1997[2] , p. 104-5).

It should also be mentioned that Marti is opposed to mercantilism, consumerism and the predominance of material over spiritual life. We can see a change of axis in Marti's concerns, in which the *other* for Latin America is no longer fundamentally Europe, but rather "the giants with the seven-league boots" of North America, called by Marti simply "the seven-league giant" (MARTI, 1993, p. 121), the intellectual is critical of the monopolistic and protectionist policies of the United States:

> Jose Marti had already warned of the US tendency to extend its dominance over Latin America, for which the US needed to control Cuba and Puerto Rico, objectives achieved in 1898 with the defeat and withdrawal of Spain from its last two colonies in Latin America. The US thus managed to prevent them from falling under British domination, as was the case with the rest of the continent, and at the same time began its empire in the Latin American area (SADER, 1985, p. 10).

Martin's criticism was aimed at the North American standard of modernity and economic and social development, which, more or less subtly, was also desired by Latin American intellectuals and political leaders. With the intention of protecting Latin America, US president James Monroe, in 1823, proposed his doctrine that would characterize any attempt by a European nation to introduce itself politically or economically into any country on the American continent as an aggression against the US. However,

> This defense was "purely moral", because it did not correspond to the real capacity of the US to intervene in the politics of the continent. At that time, the capacity for political and military influence was limited at most to the Caribbean region. In any case, the Monroe Doctrine served as an ideological justification for the US expansion westwards and the consequent massacre of the indigenous populations. (...) In 1889, (...) the US convened the First Pan-American Conference in Washington. This conference marked a practical attempt by the US to assume effective leadership over the direction of the continent, proposing as a concrete interest in Pan-Americanist ideological propaganda, a customs union that would remove the commercial influence of England and other European countries, in favor of US commercial interests. This proposal was not realized due to the vehement opposition of some countries such as Argentina and Chile (SANTOS, 2010,

p. 3).

This imperialist stance is incisively criticized and denied by Marti, especially in his essay *Nuestra America,* among others, in which he crystallizes and completely assumes the existence of two Americas (RODRIGUEZ, 2006). With this, Marti suggests a proper path for Latin America, a path that corresponds to its historical originality: "la America nueva!" (MARTI, 1993, p. 127)[8] . With this, "Marti became the 'apostle' who symbolizes the historical greatness and creative vocation of an intrepid and inventive people" (FERNANDES, 1995).

It is therefore possible to admit that in Darcy Ribeiro we find a revival of the major and significant ideals expressed by Simon Bolivar and Jose Marti, even proposing, according to Ronaldo C. Aguiar (1996), as a consequence of the presence of these characters in Darcy Ribeiro's thinking: "it is 'very likely' that, in the future, a 'supranational political entity' will even emerge, where Latin Americans will finally 'live out their destiny'" (AGUIAR, 1996, p. 26).

[8] It should also be mentioned that "Marti strives to construct and use the concept of culture as the matrix of Latin Americanism. Thus, he claims Latin American uniqueness, the cultural authority of intellectuals, as the normative axis of the Latin American *us*, a discourse that implies a criticism of the modernizing project of the United States, based more on the economy than on culture and the totality of society" (VELOSO, 2011, p. 142).

Chapter ii - influential arguments

2.1 Radical thinking

As we tried to elucidate earlier, it is possible to recognize in Darcy Ribeiro an "heir, in his own way, to the ideals of 'Patria Grande' and 'Nuestra America' of Simon Bolivar and Jose Marti respectively" (MIGLIEVICH- RIBEIRO, 2013, p. 55), which marked him in his theoretical elaborations and reflections on Latin America. In addition to both the Venezuelan and the Cuban, Darcy also turned enthusiastically to other, closer sources of Brazilian origin.

In 1984, Darcy Ribeiro published an essay in issue 2 of *Revista do Brasil* entitled "Manoel Bomfim, antropologo" (Manoel Bomfim, anthropologist), which was later added in 1993 as the opening of the reissue of Manoel Bomfim's book, *America Latina: males de origem (Latin America: evils of origin*), originally published in 1905. But the appreciation and impact of reading Bomfim's book on Darcy occurred years earlier. Darcy himself reported that, during his first exile in Montevideo, he spent a long time researching in Uruguayan public libraries, reading everything he could get his hands on on the subject of *Latin America, with* the aim of starting to write his *Studies in the Anthropology of Civilization.* It was during this period of intense reading and reflection that he was able to break away from what he called the "simplistic" and overly regionalist perspective that he had brought with him to realize that the Brazilian reality is part of a larger whole: Latin America.

[9] This was a Brazilian magazine founded in 1916 by Julio de Mesquita with the aim of serving as a place for literary writers and promoting discussions about the context of the First World War, which was then underway. It had five specific phases: In the first phase, from 1916 to 1925, the magazine was run by Mesquita himself and by Monteiro Lobato, who bought it in 1918; transforming it into a place to promote his works and those of other authors. In 1925, Lobato, then in financial difficulties, sold the magazine to Assis Chateaubriand. In the second phase, in 1926, the magazine opened a space for discussions between conservatives and modernists. But in 1927 the magazine was closed down. In its third phase, in 1938, Chateaubriand reactivated the magazine to act as a voice against the Estado Novo. However, this chronological period of the magazine is also seen as elitist and liberal, although progressive intellectuals also participated. In the fourth phase, in 1943, the magazine was discontinued and, in 1944, Chateaubriand republished it with a different approach with the aim of making it a competitor to Revista Selegoes, but the venture didn't last a year. Finally, in its last and fifth phase, from 1984 to 1990, the periodical functioned as a

space for the articulation of political and social ideas, and it was a period of fragmented but significant publications. However, despite the lack of constancy in the publication of its issues, it can be considered a period of excellence for the magazine, because, among other reasons, it was during this phase that Darcy Ribeiro was in charge (Cf.: LUCA, 1996; 2012).

For Adelia Miglievich-Ribeiro (2013), this break with a "provincial" past in the years of exile helped Darcy to recognize himself as a "Latin American citizen", or as Darcy himself liked to be called, a "Latin American Brazilian" (ZEA, 1993, p. 100). 100) and gave him an unprecedented affirmation of identity in exile, at a time when Brazilian intellectuals were trained more in Europe and the United States, with little or no identification with the history and culture of the *German* nations. From then on, Darcy Ribeiro began to develop his studies, which would lead him to rework the history of the formation of the Latin American people, as well as the utopia it contained, emphasizing the duty to "oppose what he called 'reflexive modernization', and propose 'evolutionary acceleration', based on the scientific-technological revolution, managed autonomously by each society and thus guaranteeing its emancipation" (MIGLIEVICH-RIBEIRO, 2013, p. 61). 61).

It was during this phase that Darcy Ribeiro, stimulated by his discoveries, best laid the foundations for his indignation. He didn't accept the vast majority of Latin American authors he encountered in his intense reading, who outlined an explanation of the continent's historical mismatch as "parrots of other people's wisdom or parlapatos" (RIBEIRO, 2005, p. 13), repeating speeches and theories from other hegemonic geopolitics. 13), repeating the speeches and theories of thinkers from other hegemonic geopolitics, judging and legitimizing European colonialism in their many pages, and insisting with a depressed feeling or strange enjoyment on the inferiority of our dark Latin American people, which was never confirmed historically (RIBEIRO, 2005). It is in this milieu that a novelty emerges:

> In the midst of this bibliographic maze, a light would sometimes appear. Even suns would shine there, in fleeting flickers of lucidity. But my greatest surprise, my enchantment, was to come across one day, by chance, attracted by the title, this extraordinary book, *Latin America - Evils of Origin,* by Manoel Bomfim. Reading it, I found myself in front of an original thinker, the greatest that we Latin Americans have generated. A fully mature thinker in 1905, when he published his book (RIBEIRO, 2005, p. 13).

It is possible that this position of confrontation with a *coloniality of knowledge*[10] evident in Darcy, has renewed intrepidity from the readings made of the

10 "In an interview conducted with the creative thinker and Brazilian

polymath intellectual, Darcy Ribeiro, in 1978, (...) he refers to Brazilian scientists and social scientists in particular as 'Cavalo-de-Santo', that is, as mere receptacles and reproducers of the theses constructed and provided by intellectuals from other geographies considered as hegemonic centers of Bomfim's text. There is no doubt that "Darcy Ribeiro inherited his singsong social thought from Bomfim" (MIGLIEVICH-RIBEIRO, 2013, p. 63). For there was, as we have said, evidence in Bomfim's time of the Portuguese preference for appearance, or mere imitation, seen in the excessive use of adornments on clothing, nobiliary titles bought to stamp nobility, in some cases to covertly reinforce an idea of belonging to the nobility, fallacious genealogical trees were drawn up simulating kinship with citizens of this same nobility (FERNANDES, 2012). Likewise, the inclination towards appearance was associated with erudition, which was evidenced by reading books written by prestigious authors, but without their contents having any foundation or even the slightest connection to the reality in which they were applied. In other words, it was an erudition that was, to a large extent, merely fictional. According to Bomfim (2005), these scholars did not transmit anything new, they simply reproduced copiously what they read in books elsewhere, without even reflecting on the usefulness and legitimacy of what they read and how this acquired knowledge could be used to bring progress and full development to Latin America and Brazil.

The criticism leveled at Latin American thinkers and elites was their disregard and contempt for an autonomous posture of observation, which consequently did not cooperate here to produce a pertinent and adequate science to explain the hardships of the reality they were dealing with. This *intelligentsia*'s enjoyment was based on the knowledge they read and repeated from books, usually written by foreign authors, trying "unfortunately" to use what they understood from these westernized readings here. Bomfim (2005) condemns this ostentatious knowledge which hindered a serious science, concerned with events to be observed systematically[10][11] .

This is a vital point in Bomfim's argument, a stance deeply marked by criticism of the difficulties, or even refusal, of Latin American elites and intellectuals to consistently analyze their own reality, and moreover, to seek solutions in Europe.

For Bomfim, Latin American intellectuals were steeped in a "book culture", which was the search for an interpretation of reality in common sense or through the importation of general theories elaborated in foreign books, used as an answer to

(...) Bearing in mind that the predominant theoretical and epistemic reference point studied in our public or private universities is still, with very few exceptions, Eurocentric and North American content. It is worth questioning even which authors, texts and theories are conferred and legitimized as classics in Brazilian sociology. (...) Catherine Walsh characterizes this epistemological formation and articulation as coloniality of knowledge, and explains that this is the positioning of Eurocentrism as the only perspective of knowledge, concomitantly discarding the existence and viability of other knowledges and epistemic rationalities, as well as other knowledges that are not of the same matrix as white European or Europeanized men." (ROMERA JR, 2013, p. 87).

[11] This lack of observation was not exclusive to the people colonized here. Bomfim also pointed out this problem in the scientific studies produced by the French, as Gontijo (2003, p. 138) explains: "Bomfim considered French studies to be characterized by an absence of scientific rigour, since they presented, according to him, a reduced criterion of observation and, consequently, a poor understanding of reality. Observation criteria would therefore be necessary for a rigorously scientific study, (...) which the author considered capable of objectively guiding the study of subjectivities."

> the social reality of these countries. The mistake of these intellectuals was to take the cause as a symptom, always establishing the view enshrined in the books, perpetuating a feeling of malaise as a result of the application of these imported ideas to the Brazilian reality (BECHELLI, 2009, p. 78).

Darcy Ribeiro points out with frank sadness that, "this is an ugly sin that we continue to sin with the greatest ardor" (2005, p. 21). 21), and describes having seen young doctors in history, social sciences and philosophy who have never read or heard anything about Manoel Bomfim, and even, astonished, claims to know of anthropologists who are "even proud of never having taken the time to read Gilberto Freyre, Arthur Ramos or Josue de Castro, whom they see as mere social philosophers" (RIBEIRO, 2005, p. 21).[12] Darcy's words are incisive throughout the text and deserve to be highlighted:

> It's a sad situation, that of a people who lack explanations and even consolations for their failures, who lose the best that they have to offer in the midst of a blablabla of foreign quotations. Manoel Bomfim was so far above his peers because he had a basic ability that is his distinguishing feature: the ability to look around him, with eyes capable of seeing the evidence. The others just read, quoted. Bomfim knew perfectly well that bookish erudition is a disease of the spirit, and that a stray, merely fruitful intelligence is intrinsically unfruitful. He himself once emphasized that "there are many spirits among us who are fond of reading, but true science, which is the authentic science of observation, does not exist" (RIBEIRO, 2005, p. 18).

Bomfim is considered an avant-garde thinker. It is even possible that, like other critics[13] , Darcy also made a similar claim, suggesting that "he was way ahead of what was being written and read in that Brazil, which was even more alienated than it is today" (2005, p. 16). Now, as much as Bomfim didn't allow himself to be seduced by the racist explanations of the time that justified the backwardness of the colonized peoples, he also understood like few others the consequent political, economic and cultural atrocities resulting from the colonization process and, furthermore, conceptualized the meaning of *national identity* and the meaning of Latin America in its specificity in relation to both Europe and Anglo-Saxon America; It is a fact that his social thought, like that of any other author, at any time, despite assuming the

---

[12] This criticism of contemporary researchers and intellectuals from our America is also echoed by the Argentine philosopher Enrique Dussel, who asserts that such behavior is in itself a serious indictment of the fact that *"a certain colonialism* makes us pay attention to Europeans or North Americans, but never to Latin Americans" (DUSSEL, 1986, p. 15. Emphasis added).

[13] Examples include: Maria T. Nunes (1997), in writing a text introducing one of the books that express Bomfim's greatest intellectual maturity, *O Brasil na America;* another, a short essay by Dante Moreira Leite (1992) in which he relates Bomfim's work to the affirmation of the unprotected classes; finally, Evaristo de Moraes Filho (1993), in writing a few words for the ears of the book *A América Latina: males* de *origem.*

configuration of a *counter-discourse,* was absolutely inserted in the historical, cultural and intellectual field of his time (AGUIAR, 1996). It's not without reason that Bomfim espouses the positivist belief that was winning over minds and hearts - the most progressive, by the way - at the beginning of the 20th century.

If we think about the *classic* authors and works that gave scientific support to sociology in its genesis, such as Emile Durkheim, Max Weber and Karl Marx, it becomes clear that not even they were "ahead of their time"; on the contrary, they observed reality and reflected on it. According to Ronaldo Aguiar (2000), these authors reflected on the context in front of them, analyzing it critically, antagonizing the theoretical and conceptual frameworks that had dominated until then. These *classics* were able to transcend the era in which they lived precisely because they observed and interpreted the world in a radically[14] different way, constructing an innovative reflection on the issues of their day, extending their critical ideas and concepts into the times that follow. In other words, it would be a false impression to believe that they were "outside" history. They weren't.

> The genius of the classics was not in their supposed timelessness. It was, above all, in their ability to understand the intricacies of the empirical reality of their time, extracting from it the links that mediate between the essential and the apparent, between the lasting and the temporary. (...) Manoel Bomfim lived exactly his historical moment, he thought about the same problems that afflicted his generation (...). The truth is that Manoel Bomfim elaborated *a particular and differentiated intellectual synthesis - using as a frame of reference the same historical, social, cultural and political elements made available to the other intellectuals of his time.* In short, the thought and work of Manoel Bomfim (with all its virtues and contradictions) is perfectly inscribed within the intellectual field of his time, differentiating itself, however, as a *counter-discourse* (or as a *critical discourse),* from the dominant ideological discourse, to which, with its own singularity, nuances and characteristics, the work and thought of the majority of his peers were tied (AGUIAR, 2000, p. 33-4. Emphases added).

Not only is conservative thought legitimately a child of its time, but so is radical thought. One of the benefits of radical thinking, according to Antonio Candido (1990), is its ability to expose the depths of the conservative mentality, its genesis and the ways in which it spreads: "the Brazilian would be a man made conservative by the social and cultural inheritance derived from the despoiling mentality of the Colony" (CANDIDO, 1990, p. 13).

---

[14] Antonio Candido applies this classification to Manoel Bomfim, stating that he "was a *permanent radical,* who analyzed the foundations of Brazilian and Latin American society with harshness, in addition to the work regime" (1990, p. 10. Emphasis added). Ronaldo C. Aguiar (2000), in his book *O Rebelde Esquecido* (*The Forgotten Rebel*), dedicates an entire chapter to this theme, entitled, *Um modo radical de pensar (A radical way of thinking).* This emblematic stance and reading of Bomfim's life and work influenced the subtitle of this chapter.

There have been many tributes, honors and certificates of singularity and prestige awarded to Bomfim, or denied to him, according to some, with total injustice. Cleiton Neves (2008) claims that Bomfim was one of the first theorists to value mestipagem, preceded only by Jose Marti and Jose Enrique Rodo. What's more, "his relevance lies in the singularity of his thought in the history of ideas in Brazil - which did not have a tradition of thinkers concerned with the Latin American theme" (NEVES, 2008, p. 3). Teresa Malatian (1996) classifies Bomfim as one of the forerunners of the intellectuals who thought of the state as the central character of progress and modernization, developing theories to strengthen national states. Following in the footsteps of the precursors, Maria Nunes places the master from Sergipe as "one of the first Brazilian scholars to make the distinction between culture and race, a common confusion among us until the flowering of cultural anthropology" (1997, p. 20).

It is worth highlighting the assertion of Ronaldo C. Aguiar, who published the book *O Rebelde Esquecido: tempo, vida e obra de Manoel Bomfim (The Forgotten Rebel: time, life and work of Manoel Bomfim), a* text derived from his doctoral thesis, which was awarded the Prize for Best Doctoral Thesis at the 1st CNPq-ANPOCS Brazilian Competition of Scientific Works and University Theses in Social Sciences, in 1999. Emphasizing that his *sociological biography* would be, above all, "paying homage to Manoel Bomfim, who, (...) - I hope! - will be recognized for what he truly is: one of Brazil's most important and lucid social thinkers" (AGUIAR, 2000, p. 23).

There are those, like Azevedo Amaral, who say that they are *overwhelmed* by the honor that has been bestowed upon them and, therefore, have no intention of prefacing Bomfim's *A América Latina*, since this book, "is one of those whose inexhaustible lucidity makes any explanatory comments superfluous" (2005, p. 31); and he said this in 1938, just six years after Bomfim's death. Darcy Ribeiro was no exception; contrary to Bomfim's long marginalization on the Brazilian and Latin American intellectual scene, he placed him as "the great interpreter of the process of formation of the Brazilian people" (RIBEIRO, 2005, p. 15). However, he went even further, describing him as "the *founder of* the anthropology of Brazil and Brazilians" (RIBEIRO, 2005, p. 20. Emphasis added).

But the aspect that stands out the most, or in Darcy's own words (2005), that he *identifies with the most*, is his opposition to all thinkers, whether ancient or modern, who are in league with interest groups that insist on keeping the Brazilian nation backward. An admirable capacity for indignation is combined with an undeniable sense of hope. And this characteristic, more than any other, probably imbued Darcy with the certainty that *this is a viable country,* Bomfim's conviction, which became his own, "that we will build a solidary and beautiful civilization here, as soon as we take the power of decision out of the hands of our infecund and unfaithful ruling classes" (RIBEIRO, 2005, p. 20). Darcy read Bomfim's work as an adventure in search of a utopia. Bomfim rejected adhering to and justifying the ideas and ideologies of the elites and intellectuals. His priority was a larger contingent of ignorant ex-citizens, despised mestigos and illiterate whites, cultivating the utopia of redeeming them through quality public education[15] . According to Bomfim:

> *Utopia... Utopia...* repeats common sense, Utopia, yes; let's be utopians, let's be good utopians; let's not sterilize our ideal by expecting its realization from any force immanent to utopia itself; let's be utopians, as long as we work. Without the utopians of yesteryear, men would still be living in caves today, miserable and naked. It was the utopians who drew the lines of the first city. Beneficial realities emerge from generous dreams. Utopia is the beginning of all progress and the blueprint for a better future (2005, p. 382. Emphasis added).

Darcy wasn't a utopian, he was a utopian, and a utopian in the manner of Bomfim, from whom he learned. Ronaldo Aguiar (2000) exemplifies this extraordinary relationship - and so does Darcy - in which Bomfim believed in utopia, but called himself a utopian and not merely a utopian. He knew exactly what he was saying: while the utopian doesn't have his feet on the ground or even his hands in a real world, the utopian, according to Bomfim, followed by Darcy, wants to change and transform society through a *pedagogical* dedication that is concrete and fully consistent and conscious[16] . Thus, Darcy states:

> Like Manoel Bomfim, I also believe that popular education has an indispensable role to play in our efforts to improve ourselves. Only through it will we be able to ensure that the Brazilians of tomorrow manifest their extraordinary creativity, not only in soccer and carnival, but in all human forms of expression (RIBEIRO, 2005, p. 20).

---

[15] For a discussion on the question of education in Manoel Bomfim's thought, see: Claudia V. A. P. da Silva (2012), *Contribuigao de Manoel Bomfim a educagao brasileira;* Ronaldo C. Aguiar (2000), *O rebelde esquecido,* pp. 175-198, 257-286; Ricardo S. Bechelli (2009), *Nacionalismos anti-racistas,* pp. 57-106.

[16] It is worth adding the emphasis indicated by Candido A. Gomes: "The utopia expressed by Darcy Ribeiro was to offer full-time education and full-time schools, as in Uruguay, (...) and in developed countries such as Japan and the United States. (...) There is no discussion about whether the school should be full-time or not, *or* whether *it is a school or not"* (2010, p. 57. Emphasis added).

However, it should be mentioned that Darcy Ribeiro is not entirely passive to Manoel Bomfim's ideas. In an emblematic way, we can mention two issues that are relevant to this research: firstly, a "sociological biologism"[17] as Darcy points out (2005, p. 19). Darcy's criticism is not severe, but it does make explicit a certain antagonism in Bomfim's formulations, who has made an effort to censure biologist sociologies, yet insists on theorizing from a biologism. But what has been indicated as criticism can also be placed as praise, because the persistence in the use of the organicist metaphorical resource is due, above all, to the ability it demonstrates to generalize in a complex sense, which recognizes the specificity of the object studied and, at the same time, integrates it into the totality of the universe[18] . In this sense, Darcy Ribeiro

[17] The concept of "social parasitism" is a key category for Bomfim's socio-historical explanation, especially since the use of the organicist metaphor is evident and closely linked to his training in medicine, as some suggest (cf.: AGUIAR, 2000, p. 300-15; MALATIAN, 1996, p. 114-19; FERNANDES, 2012, p. 105).

[18] Bomfim himself was fully aware of the metaphorical use in his organicist language, as he reports: "Poor Darwin! Never did he suppose that his brilliant work could serve as a justification for the crimes and villainies of slavers and Indian executioners! (...) Darwin never pretended that the law of natural selection applied to the human species, as the theorists of egoism and rapaciousness claim. He recognized that living beings struggle for life; but this expression 'struggle' does not have, in his theory, the narrow meaning to which they reduce bashful spirits; *struggle for life* means, for him, the tendency to live, the effort to preserve life and propagate it, and not simply material conflict, cruel aggression" (BOMFIM, 2005, p. 275. Emphasis added). It should be mentioned that theorizing society as an organism is not unique to Manoel Bomfim, as comparisons and biological arguments were already widely used by social scientists of the time, influenced mainly by naturalism and evolutionism. It's worth remembering that Bomfim's theses were also close to some of Emile Durkheim's arguments - especially in *Da Divisao do Trabalho Social* - for whom the biological became a model for analyzing and understanding social facts; it's true that Bomfim doesn't quote Durkheim, but in fact his text suggests that he was familiar with the French sociologist's work, as Ortiz (1985, p. 23) commented on this: "from the analogy between biology and society comes the notion of disease, a key concept for understanding Latin American backwardness". Marx also makes use of this organicist resource at various moments and argues that, "the communal regime would have restored to the social body all the forces hitherto absorbed by the state *parasite*, which feeds on society and obstructs its free movement" (2011, p. 59. Emphasis added); and states that governments, in their despotism of capital over labor, constitute, "the condition of their own *parasitic* existence" (2011, p. 78. Emphasis added). At another point, Marx and Engels state that, "[i]n commercial crises (...) a social *epidemic* breaks out which in previous epochs would have seemed absurd - the *epidemic* of overproduction", and furthermore, "the bourgeoisie is (...) incapable of domination because it is (...) unable to dominate.) is incapable of domination because it is incapable of ensuring the existence of its slave in his slavery, because it is obliged to let him fall into a situation where he must *feed him instead of being fed by him"* (2005, p. 71, 78. Emphasis added). Therefore, Manoel Bomfim's concept of parasitism, more than a language taken from biology (going beyond Darcy Ribeiro's analysis), was an instrument for interpreting social life, whose ascendancy in Marx's ideas was evident: "This influence, of a general nature, of the parasitism of the metropolises on the organism of the colonies, reaches all the manifestations of collective life in its fourfold aspect: economic, political, social and moral. (...) It is the economic effects that are the most sensitive in this regime of parasitic colonization. One could even say that they are the primary effects, to which the others are linked as secondary effects. In itself, the parasitism of metropolises, like social parasitism in general, is an economic phenomenon whose effects are reflected in the whole of social life" (BOMFIM, 2005, p. 143). It is important to emphasize that more recently there have been calls for a conceptual reconfiguration of knowledge, the validation of which is supposed to depend on the pertinent confrontation of the questions posed to them. The migration of concepts between different types of knowledge, when producing science, no longer carries the negative charge it once did. Faced with the ramifications and plural redefinitions that contemporaneity seems to give rise to, it doesn't

(2005) adds that the concept of "social parasitism" is above all a language or paradigm, through which, expressing himself with evident, visible and explainable elements, Bomfim used them as allegories to explain the hiddenness of the invisible national being.

Secondly, there is divergence in the understanding of the category *Latin America.* Ronaldo Aguiar (2000) explains that, in its early days, this category was part of a geo-ideological discourse aimed at supporting French interests. By privileging the category as a kind of unifying political "symbol", Napoleon III's France intended to set the Latin American peoples against the Germanic, Anglo-Saxon and Slavic peoples. The aim was to establish a possible cultural, linguistic and ethnic identity for the *Latins,* thus overcoming national or even continental borders and allowing for French aggregation of the whole. In other words, Napoleon III's strategy sought to "globalize" the Latin peoples under the hegemony of France.

Bomfim was emphatically opposed to this. He argued that the term Latin America had no unifying support in reality. On the contrary, he argued that,

> The rest of us - Argentines, Peruvians, Brazilians, Chileans... who are so-called *Latin Americans,* never think of *Latin America.* For our concepts of reality, in the simple positive sense of common relations, or as the convergence of any immediate action, there is no such unity. (...) Any foreigner who has lived here with us will talk about - Venezuela, Paraguay, Mexico, Nicaragua... but will never feel the need to focus their minds on this concept - *Latin America.* On the other hand, all those who don't know us, if they are theory-makers with a tongue in social, historical or political matters, do not fail to repeat emphatic and puerile prejudices about the unreal unity of Latin America (BOMFIM, 1997, p. 31. Emphasis added).

Manoel Bomfim, in his time, became aware that the widespread use of the category Latin America became an ideological ruse of the elites of the time, who, in agreement with the neo-colonial interests of the former European metropolises, sought to complicate heterogeneous nations in order to demean them as *sovereign national units.* In this sense, according to Bomfim, the perception of the existence of a Latin America would mean nothing more than a "'condemnatory epithet' and not a positive reference to a *politically and culturally constituted unit"* (AGUIAR, 1996, p. 26,

sound like a methodological lacuna to borrow from the repertoire of other knowledges. Recent and timely studies, such as those by Maturana and Varela (2001), Edgar Morin (2005; 2010), Joao B. Libaneo (2002), Roberia Nascimento (2007), or Hugo Assmann (1998), reflect the positive reception of conceptual migration and its new interpretations by the scientific community. This seems compatible with the proposal for hybrid research that can reaffirm the need for plural, complex and democratic knowledge.

emphasis added). Contrasting this thesis, Darcy Ribeiro, in addition to reaffirming the existence of a Latin America, as "cultural uniformity and promising to achieve its socio-political and economic unity tomorrow" (RIBEIRO, 1996, p. 22), also tries to demonstrate that this unity derived from convergent civilizing processes, leading to "the formation of a group of peoples, not only unique in relation to the world, but also increasingly homogeneous" (RIBEIRO, 1996, p. 23). However, it is worth remembering that:

> Basically, there are visible similarities between Manoel Bomfim and Darcy Ribeiro in terms of identifying the problem and the fact that they both defended progressive positions. They differed, however, in terms of their approach and other proposals for overcoming the problem. And it couldn't be any other way. After all, both authors (and not just them: all of them) are inseparable from the intellectual, historical and political environment in which they thought and wrote their work (AGUIAR, 2000, p. 481).

2. 2 From a Victorian in the tropics

Another significant contribution to Darcy Ribeiro's thinking comes from the Pernambuco social scientist and writer Gilberto Freyre (1900-1987). This reference remains implicit, especially in a preface written by Darcy Ribeiro for a Venezuelan edition of *Casa-Grande & Senzala (CG&S),* presented by the Ayacucho Library in 1977; the text was later included in *Ensaios Insolitos*^[9] , along with other texts on Brazilian culture; finally, it was republished in a paperback edition in 1997, the year Darcy Ribeiro died.

It is interesting to mention that this last publication of his preface was made at the request of Darcy himself, when he was asked about the publication of a collection of essays by him. When Darcy agreed to the publication, he suggested that, in addition to the selected texts, one of "his favorites" should be included (RIBEIRO, 1997[3] , p. 5), i.e. his prologue: *Gilberto Freyre: An Introduction to Casa-Grande & Senzala.* The eloquence with which Darcy writes this *introduction,* as well as his predilection for it, makes it clear how important Gilberto Freyre's work is in his reflections. Our anthropologist reflects, after a stimulating introduction, on the following items: the writer; the interpreter; the method; the protagonists; the Indian and the Jesuit; the Brazilian manor and the Negro; ending with a biochronology. This range of aspects alone would make for a more in-depth analysis; however, we have dared to highlight just a few points that elucidate the purpose of this chapter.

According to Haydee R. Coelho (2000), in the prefaces in which Darcy comments on both works and their authors, it is possible to see that by talking about others, he also introduces his own voice into the text. In other words, by using other people's language, he was able to express his convictions and thoughts: "In listening to others, he becomes listened to" (COELHO, 2000, p. 142). [19]

It's worth noting that, contrary to Darcy Ribeiro, Freyre had no sympathy for Manoel Bomfim's approaches. For Darcy, this was unacceptable, since Gilberto Freyre and his contemporaries had "a domestic fountain of pure water" (RIBEIRO, 2005, p. 18), and they despised it, preferring to develop their concepts and theories from a Bomfimian anthropological perspective[20] and a foreign one. Darcy Ribeiro (2005), as if apologizing for his criticism of Freyre (or in irony), goes so far as to say that Gilberto, having a vast culture, would certainly not have read the works of the master from Sergipe, suggesting that Gilberto's genius and intelligence would not allow the greatness of Manoel Bomfim to go unnoticed.

This interpretation is absolutely wrong. It is known that Gilberto had full access to Manoel Bomfim's works, as historian Claudio Marcio Coelho (2007, p. 107-8) makes clear:

> In 1919, Freyre was at *Baylor University* when he became a social correspondent for the *Diario de Pernambuco,* where he wrote articles on social, cultural, political and regional issues. Freyre was concerned about the intellectual clashes in Brazil and the challenges of building a national identity, *so he kept up to date with Brazilian social thought in the works of authors such as* Euclides da Cunha, Nina Rodrigues, Sylvio Romero, *Manoel Bonfim,* (...) among others (emphasis added).

---

[19] RIBEIRO, Darcy. *Insolite Essays.* Porto Alegre: L&PM, 1979.

[20] Here is a reference to the American anthropologist Franz Boas, who had a recognized influence on Gilberto: "Freyre (...) met Franz Boas through Oliveira Lima and decided to study at *Columbia University* (New York), where he began his master's studies (...).In 1922, Freyre recorded in his diary that he considered it important to study the early works of his master's oldest disciples: Wissler and Kroeber. (...) Freyre showed great appreciation for Boas. He admired his anthropological pioneering spirit in thorough, exhaustive, empathetic and systematic field research. He also appreciated his scientific agnosticism and aversion to abstract theorizing, as well as his preference for description over generalizations in Boasian anthropology. (...) Franz Boas had a decisive influence on Freyre's intellectual formation." (COELHO, 2007, p. 84, 85, 89, 90). In the words of Gilberto Freyre (2003, p. 31): "Professor Franz Boas is the master figure of whom the greatest impression has remained with me to this day. I met him during my first days at Columbia. I don't think any Russian student of the Romantics of the 19th century was more intensely concerned about the fate of Russia than I was about the fate of Brazil at the time I met Boas. It was as if everything depended on me and those of my generation; on our way of resolving age-old issues. And of the Brazilian problems, none worried me as much as that of miscegenation."

Gilberto Freyre read Bomfim's work, but preferred to disqualify it, going so far as to label this theorist from Sergipe as a *"pamphleteer"* and even, in his greatest work, *Casa-Grande & Senzala,* refers to him as *an "Indianophile to the root of his hair" (apud* BECHELLI, 2009, p. 107). Freyre was more vigorously focused on the theories he had absorbed in the United States and Europe; Bomfim's hostile arguments against the so-called "parasitic" colonizers without further concessions and his exaltation, above all, of the indigenous and Afro labor force in Latin America provoked in Freyre an irrepressible rejection[21] .

In addition to this contrast between Northeastern authors, Darcy Ribeiro had always been a confessed admirer of Gilberto Freyre's work; he even "took some inspiration from him for *The Brazilian People",* as Maria L. Pallares-Burke and Peter Burke (2009, p. 320) suggested. However, he did not nurture his admiration without careful criticism; for example, in his aforementioned *O Povo Brasileiro,* he absolutely rejected the idea of "racial democracy". According to Darcy Ribeiro, the peculiar form of Brazilian racism that boasts morenity does not get rid of the heavy "burden of oppression, prejudice and anti-black discrimination that it contains"; as well as the "very expectation that the black man disappears through mestigagem (which) is a racism" (RIBEIRO, 1995, p. 225-6. The parenthesis is ours).

However, beyond any criticism, for Darcy Ribeiro, the master of Apipucos[22] "wrote, in fact, the most important work of Brazilian culture" (RIBEIRO, 1997[3] , p. 8); an impression that permeates his entire *introduction* to *CG&S.* Ribeiro goes so far as

---

[21] Another possible reason for Freyre's preference for foreign authors over national ones is clarified by, "Physical and at the same time mystical love is what, in his own words, Gilberto Freyre felt towards England. (...) Much in England seduced Freyre: the language, the history, the behavior of the English are just a small sample of what he loved.(...) Much in England seduced Freyre: the language, the history, the behavior of the English, their humor, their phlegm and their eccentricity are just a small sample of the object of his love. (...) However, more than any other, the greatest reason for Freyre's fascination with Oxford and England seems to be that there he visualized a Brazil in reverse. In many respects, precisely in what was most opposite to his own country, Oxford came to represent a possible Brazil (...) It was another sensibility and another culture that he discovered there and that came to guide his image of an ideal country" (ALLARES-BURKE, 1997, p. 13-21). The strange lack of prudence and sensitivity went so far as to make it possible that, according to Pallares-Burke, "Gilberto Freyre never experienced any resentment towards the English. As happens with lovers, one might think that Freyre's eyes, 'clouded' by the love he felt, as he once confessed, never wanted to see anything that could shake his attachment to the land of his 'dear Englishman Mr. Williams'. (...) On at least two occasions, when he was disappointed by the behaviour of the English, Freyre's reaction reveals his idealization of the English as a person of solid character: the vices could only be due to the corrupting influence of the Brazilian environment" (1997, p. 35).

[22] *Mestre de Apipucos* refers to the neighborhood where Gilberto Freyre lived since 1941, when he bought and had restored the small big house of Engenho Dois Irmaos, in Apipucos - Recife (PE). When he died in 1987, the house and its surroundings became the headquarters of the Gilberto Freyre Foundation. A documentary about his life was released with this title in 1959, directed by Joaquim Pedro de Andrade: *O Mestre de Apipucos,* Documentario (1959) 8min. (Available at: https://www.youtube.com/watch?v=-QGeR5Pco4Y).

to reread some of the criticisms in reverse, such as the fact that, *a priori,* Gilberto Freyre does not have a specific theoretical method[23] ; which would not be enough to detract from his extensive essay, since what there is is a plurality of methods, or in another more radical way: "there is simply no method. (...) [and furthermore] none of the classic works of social sciences can be explained by their methodological virtues. Quite the opposite" (RIBEIRO, 1997[3] , p. 42). He goes on to exemplify that everything that has been written with too much methodological rigor has resulted in *mediocrity.* Therefore, *CG&S* becomes emblematic in the first category, pointing out outstanding contributions to science, "which become classic books that we should all read for the flavor they give us of new and fresh knowledge" (RIBEIRO, 19973, p. 43).

Other commentators on Freyre (ARAUJO, 2009; FONSECA, 2007; SOUZA, 2000) have observed that the paradigm of ambiguity and contradiction that constituted Freyre's early writings - praised by Darcy - was replaced in maturity by a spirit of a closed system, a compilation of certainties and suggestions for practical and political intervention. Souza (2000), the most inquisitive, summarizes: "What is certain is that Freyre's mature work is a kind of caricature of his youthful work" (p. 70), attributing this to political opportunism or personal vanity, generating a hardening, a closing of horizons and perspectives[24] :

> In fact, Gilberto Freyre concludes his mature work. He concludes by transforming some of his brilliant youthful intuitions about the specificity and uniqueness of Brazilian social formation into a nationalist and Luso-imperialist ideology of dubious democratic potential. What had previously taken the form of wondering about the peculiarities and transformations of a European culture in the tropics was transformed into "tropicology", a set of assertions of dubious scientificity, laden with impressionism, but easily used as a unitary ideology of the "tropical and mestizo". An ideology of "erasing differences" (SOUZA, 2000, p. 70)[25] .

[23] Cf.: Debora Gerstenberger (2014); Peter Burke (1997); Maria L. Pallares-Burke & Peter Burke (2009).

[24] Perhaps this explains the point made by Edson Nery da Fonseca, who, when dealing with criticism of Freyre's work, cites an interview in which Darcy Ribeiro allegedly said that his book *Sociologia: introdugao ao estudo de seus principios*, released in 1945, was "worthless" (FONSECA, 2007, p. 264). It's difficult to assimilate this information since Fonseca doesn't give us any clues about the interview (when? where? to whom?). We don't know the rhythm of the interview, the context of either the question or the supposed answer. At most, if we take advantage of this note, we can attribute it to a Freyre perceived by Darcy as the opposite of the one whose creativity and style he so appreciated.

[5] It is necessary to clarify that: "The separation between the works of 'youth' and 'maturity' is not made in order to demonstrate any 'epistemological cut' in the author. Freyre is the same holistic thinker, who thinks of society as an organic whole based on parts that complete each other. (...) However, for the hermeneutic and interpretative effort, it makes a big difference whether we are talking about potentialities inscribed in a society of the 16th and 17th centuries, such as Brazil. XVI and XVII, such as the Brazil of *Casa-grande e senzala,* or the supposed characteristics of a nation in the middle of the second half of the 20th century, as in the case of texts dealing with luso-tropicology" (SOUZA, 2000, p. 71).

Darcy also realizes this. When he compares, for example, the works *CG&S* and *Sobrados e Mocambos,* with a later one, in this case *Ordem e Progressed*[6] , he points out that in this one, to the detriment of those, "he tries to obey a plan as rigorous as possible for an undisciplined and anarchic nature such as his", which didn't appease the criticism he had suffered, on the contrary, the result, "was a book of inferior quality that cannot be compared to the first two" (RIBEIRO, 1997[3] , p. 43). This further underlines the importance and significance of the *classic* work to Darcynian thought.

The approximations that can be made between Darcy and Freyre go beyond academic "borders". Even if it's not necessarily a reciprocal influence. One of these is the question of admiration. Not only did he literally claim to be his admirer, but this was a characteristic that they both nurtured, a self-confessed vanity. In his own words, Darcy says: "Like me, he likes to be puffed up. He savors compliments like candy" (1997[3] , p. 7). As Helena Bomeny reminds us, the anthropologist from Minas Gerais didn't dispense with any compliments, in many ritualistic academic moments, when someone was meant to introduce him at the respective ceremonies, making the initial use of the, almost refrain, "Professor Darcy Ribeiro dispenses with introductions", then he would quickly burst out: "I don't, you can say everything about me that the public might know" (BOMENY, 2001, p.33). Darcy even wrote the assertion in an ironic but humorous text entitled "Louvapoes":

> Many people say I'm unbearably proud, even vain. That's true. So what? I'm full of reasons for being proud of what I've done all my life. I always repeat that the modest are right, everyone knows for himself. (...) [and so he adds] Why do I need so much for the people around me or who see me from afar to praise me without tiring? I confess that I need and like compliments too much *(apud* BOMENY, 2001, p. 33).

Another approximation is that Darcy, after pointing out that *CG&S* was "the most important work written about Brazilian culture" (RIBEIRO, 19973, p. g), asserts that it is too closely linked to its author, and that inevitably, "it is very difficult[26] to generalize about Gilberto" (RIBEIRO, 1997[3] , p. 13). This is because both Gilberto and Darcy themselves are complex authors.

Journalist Zuenir Ventura, in an attempt to honor Darcy on his death, wrote a

[26] This book was published late, originally in 1957, and completes the trilogy proposed by Freyre: *Casa-Grande & Senzala* (originally published in 1933); *Sobrados e Mocambos* (originally published in 1936); and finally, *Ordem e Progresso.*

chronicle for the *Jornal do Brasil,* lucidly conveying this idea: "He was a blessed counter-sense, a fascinating spirit of contradiction" *(apud* BOMENY, 2001, p. 36). Following this path, Helena Bomeny (2001) intends, in her study of Darcy Ribeiro, to begin to unravel this complexity or, at least, as she outlines in the chapters of her work, to contribute with suggestions of more and more connections, thus making it possible to advance a little further in the understanding between author and "doings", highlighting the work of the educator she calls the last exponent of the "New School".

Returning to Gilberto Freyre, it is not without reason that Jesse de Souza (2000) called him the most complex, difficult and contradictory of all Brazilian thinkers. Let's mention the question that Darcy asked himself more than once in his prologue:

> The question that arises is how can the noble boy from the Freyres; the Anglo boy from Recife; the elitist moço who travels to the United States wanting to become a Protestant in order to be more American; the cabinet officer of a reactionary governor - how can he - apparently so unfit for this task, come up with the airy and beautiful interpretation of Brazilian colonial life that is *CG&S.* The fact is astonishing, but as it is undeniable, we have to live with it and explain it or at least understand it, if possible (19973, p. 12).

Gilberto Velho, for his part, is cautious in this respect, and states that "care must also be taken to avoid simplifications and schematisms in order to understand such a complex life and work" (2008, p. 15)[27] . Darcy Ribeiro will return to this question at another point. In his provisional answer to the question of what allowed Gilberto Freyre to write *CG&S,* it becomes clear that "the predominant reason is that he was ambiguous" (RIBEIRO, 19973, p. 26). On the one hand, Darcy found in Freyre an evocative sense of a familiar world, in other words, that of a Pernambuco, regional outlook. On the other hand, he had a strong Anglo-French preference, but this helped him to look at the trivial, the everyday - and as such lacking interest, novelty - with a strange, foreign, inquisitive gaze, and even more so, as an interpreting researcher. Darcy's observation even served as a stimulus for Gilbertian researchers to develop their research, as in the case of Maria Pallares-Burke who, after highlighting Darcy's notes on an "English" and a "Pernambuco" Gilberto, states that her study is an "attempt to develop and substantiate, to give substance to these valuable

27 In an interview, when Freyre was described as a man of nuance, of shades, because he doesn't like pure quantities or straight lines, he replied: "I don't know if I'm being interpreted correctly by those who say I'm a man of shades. Rather, I'm a man of paradoxes. I believe very much in the truth that paradoxes present. I think that almost all truths lie in paradoxes. I am frankly paradoxical and, as a result, I tend to scandalize the right-thinking" (FREYRE, 2010, p. 177). In addition: "Gilberto Freyre's life and production are, as he himself made a point of saying, extremely complex and necessarily contradictory." (VELHO, 2008, p. 16).

suggestions" (2005, p. 40)[28] .

Although his writing maintains a humorous tone throughout the *introduction,* Darcy Ribeiro did not spare any serious and pertinent criticism of Freyre's *CG&S* work. In his analysis, he highlighted and scrutinized several critical points. He praised culturalism, which made it possible to relativize the superiority of one civilization over another in order to combat innumerable mockeries and subalternizations, but criticized the abstention from "judgement", as if everyone were ashamed, and it was no longer possible to call by name what has a name. Since evolutionism was expunged from anthropology as a tragic disease, we no longer pay attention to its variations, in which you don't need to defend unilinear evolutionism to know that backwardness really exists in every society "asphyxiated" by the excesses of another order and that underdevelopment is a necessary prerequisite for the development of others, imposing an eternal international dependence that can only be broken if it can be seen. The Gilbertian influence on Darcy Ribeiro is, above all, in the style of writing that he pursued most in his later works, in his passion for Brazil, not in the theoretical consequences of his frameworks. Darcy Ribeiro is, in his own way, a dialectical historical materialist, nothing could be further from Freyre's point of view.

According to Darcy Ribeiro, *CG&S* is a rare combination of well-documented scientific studies with deliberately creative and stimulating literacies. Even though he asserts a serious approach to science, it is undeniable that "it is always the writer, the stylist who commands the writing" (RIBEIRO, 1997[3] , p. 15). This has become a practically unparalleled contribution by Gilberto, "since there are no previous or subsequent studies of the same scale" (RIBEIRO, 1997[3] , p. 33). What's more, through his literary liberties, Gilberto was able to break away from the "foolish rhetorical writing that was then read as literary" (RIBEIRO, 19973, p. 17). However, it should be emphasized that such brilliance in scientific-literary symbiosis caused inevitable consequences; "some nail will have to be paid for so many advantages", which in this case, was seen countless times as the "anthropologist lets himself be deceived by the novelist", therefore, it is necessary in an attentive reading to perceive, "both the literary enjoyment and the dubious knowledge, sold as good science"

[28] Pallares-Burke's opinion should be taken into the most serious consideration, since his study, when evaluated, stood out as: "its potential for renewal is unprecedented - and I would not hesitate to state that this work, besides being the most rigorous and sophisticated I know on the subject, should undoubtedly become a true watershed in Freyrian studies" (BRAGA-PINTO, 2006, p. 282). And, not least, but exactly in this text, Pallares-Burke states that Darcy Ribeiro's *introduction* to *CG&S* is one of "the most brilliant interpretations of Freyre ever made" (2005, p. 83).

(RIBEIRO, 19973, p. 19)[29] . This lack of definition of the textual genre, and the notion of hybridity - between the scientific foundation and literary art - leads to the constitution of a "deep affinity of the subject with the environment that constitutes the object of study", in other words, "the history of Brazil that Freyre writes is exposed to the elements, in intimate contact with himself" (LARRETA and GIUCCI, 2007, p.439. Cf. also: pp. 10, 427).

It seems, as we suggest here, that this dialogue between scientific study and literary writing was also incorporated into Darcy's writing activities, and that he was thus "influenced" and developed it in his own way. His first novel, *Maira*[30] , from 1976, was preceded - and based on - his extensive and complex anthropological work. By presenting different views of the Indians from their own point of view and that of *civilized* whites, *Maira* enables a dialogue with a wide range of historical and anthropological texts, such as *Religiao e Mitologia Kadiweu* (1950), *Culturas e Linguas Indigenas do Brasil* (1957), *Uira vai ao Encontro de Maira* (1957), *Os Indios e a Civilizacao: a Integracao das Populacoes Indigenas no Brasil Moderno* (1970). He also wrote other works, such as *A Fundacao do Brasil* (1992; in collaboration with Carlos de Araujo Moreira Neto), and *O Povo Brasileiro: a formacao e o sentido do Brasil* (1995), in particular the chapter *"Enfrentamento dos mundos" (Facing the Worlds)* (Cf.: COELHO, 2012).

It's worth pointing out here that *CG&S* was, first and foremost, an influential effort to interpret Brazilian history in a new way. Freyre breaks, in a sense, with a traditional, broad and hegemonically accepted line of historical exposition, based on the biographies of great personalities or on purely formal processes. Darcy didn't

[29] Gilberto Freyre himself was aware of his achievements, going so far as to say: "What mainly am I? I think I'm a writer. A literary writer. The sociologist, the anthropologist, the historian, the social scientist, the possible thinker, are in me ancillary to the writer. (...) I am a writer - or a constant apprentice writer - who, in his attempts to capture and interpret specific aspects of the human condition, in general, through that of tropical man, especially Brazilian man, in particular, has tried to capture and interpret them from various perspectives, sometimes simultaneously. Hence the confusion, the disorder, the discontinuity that certain literary critics have found in my work. Perhaps that's why so many others don't understand what these works are, the use of scientific perspectives alongside humanist ones, as well as repetition and disorder in the expression and fixation, possibly literary, of these sometimes simultaneous perspectives: expression that would give these works, according to some critics, an artistic category or poetic quality and, according to others, would reduce them to a chaotic pile of images, neither truly scientific nor literarily suggestive. (...) The truth is, however, that, in my case, what I've been trying to be is a writer who, as a writer, makes use of his training or his knowledge - if there is such a thing - scientific - anthropological, mainly - instead of pretending to be mainly an anthropologist or sociologist or historian, or institutional thinker, so to speak. This is the case - this hybrid, flexible and somewhat anarchic condition - of various Hispanics" (FREYRE, 1968, p. 165, 178, 179).

[30] This book, which in 1978 was considered by Darcy to be his "cagula son", became his favorite work, or in his own words: "and my xodo" (RIBEIRO, 1978, p. 21).

follow the path taken by Freyre, but it certainly inspired him. Even as a teenager, Gilberto had already declared a concern with "his mission", as Claudio Coelho reports, "In his *Farewell to the College* speech, at graduation in 1917, Freyre declared that knowledge must have a 'social purpose' and that Brazil needs thinkers capable of '*seeing and observing* its problems instead of sticking to what is written in foreign books', and leaders 'capable of action'" (2007, p. 111. Emphasis added). See also: PALLARES-BURKE and BURKE, 2009, p. 15-7). A certain resonance of this thought can be found in the words of Darcy (1978, p. 21), prefacing one of his most influential works, *The Civilizing Process:*

> I published this book with a lot of fear. I feared that daring to tackle such broad and complex themes would lead me to disaster. My fear must have increased when a well-known Marxist intellectual, a reader for a major publishing house, gave a scathing review of *The Civilizing Process*. He said that the author, a Brazilian Indian ethnologist who wasn't even a Marxist, intended to do nothing less than rewrite the theory of history, which was equivalent, he thought, to inventing the moto continua. The hell I did! The only reason I didn't get flattened under that very competent opinion was because I was saved by a fit of possessed rage against all those who think that intellectuals from the underdeveloped world have to be underdeveloped too.[31]

[31] In order to deepen and clarify this theme, we suggest reading the articles by Adelia Miglievich-Ribeiro (2011; 2011[2] ; 2012), who critically analyzes some of Darcy Ribeiro's works in order to broaden the explanatory canons of modernity, demonstrating how, through Darcy's thinking, he is able to elaborate a *reading* in which the American peoples are included in the history of humanity. At the same time, it fosters a decolonizing critique in the making of the Social Sciences, breaking with geopolitical centers of knowledge that want to be hegemonic.

CHAPTER III - PROPOSED INTERPRETATION OF LATIN AMERICA

3.1. Exile as a starting point

On April 1, 1964, a military coup took place in Brazil, overthrowing the government of Joao Goulart, of which Darcy Ribeiro was Chief of Staff, and drastically changing the life of the Brazilian anthropologist. Immediately, in order to escape the forces of repression, Darcy was forced, along with other members of the Goulart government and the deposed president himself, to take refuge in the Uruguayan capital, Montevideo.

Right from the start, Darcy Ribeiro confessed that he had assumed that his exile would only last six months, but this wish was dashed as he saw the period stretch out over a much longer period. After four years in Uruguay, he decided to return to Brazil, contrary to the wishes of many. He had heard that the Federal Supreme Court (STF) had annulled the military convictions against him. He had also heard about the "Passeata dos Cem Mil" and the youthful fervor. Nobody had yet foreseen the outcome of that year with AI-5. The fact is that he returned and the military reaction could be circumvented during the three months that, as he tells it, he lived with his wife, Berta, in their borrowed apartment on Toneleros Street in Copacabana. It wasn't long before he received an arrest warrant. Accompanied by his lawyer, Wilson Mirza, he presented himself to the Superior Military Court. He wasn't arrested the same day, but days and nights of uninterrupted surveillance followed. When AI-5 came into force, it wasn't 24 hours before Darcy Ribeiro was picked up from his home and locked up *ad infinitum* without *habeas corpus* or trial. After nine months in confinement, almost miraculously, a board of officers from the Navy, where he was then being held, "acquitted" him. From there, he applied for a visa to the USA, having been invited as a visiting professor to Columbia University. He was denied a visa. At the same time, he received an invitation from the Central University of Venezuela and was granted a consular visa without any problems. He headed for Caracas. His second exile. From there to Allende's Chile. Before his fall, he was already in Lima, Peru, called to cooperate with the Velasco government. While on vacation in Portugal, he discovers cancer in one of his lungs and Darcy Ribeiro begs to be treated in Brazil. Nothing is easy, but he manages to return and undergo surgery. His six-month convalescence is watched over by the military who, as soon as they can, demand that he leave the country again. Darcy Ribeiro returned to a Peru after the fall of Velasco, where his situation was no longer desirable. He visited a few neighboring countries until he received a new job invitation and left for Mexico (MIGLIEVICH-RIBEIRO, 2014).

The choice to remain in Latin America, turning down opportunities in European destinations, for example, is described by Darcy Ribeiro as: "the wisest decision I made in my life" (RIBEIRO, 1990, p. 136), because it enabled him to undertake a kind of "intellectual reconstruction". In Europe, Darcy Ribeiro only identified his career in indigenous ethnography, confined to a "bookish office", with no interlocutors and no intention of working on national projects. By favoring his exile in Uruguay, according to his conception, this made him a more conscious Brazilian, because he was Latin American. However, for Darcy, this recognition brought him a relatively painful consequence: "today I am more widely read in Latin American countries than in Brazil" (RIBEIRO, 1990, p. 136).

The same week he arrived in Uruguay, he was hired by the *Universidad de la Republica* as a professor of Anthropology at the *Facultad de Humanidades y Ciencias de la Education*, on an exclusive basis. In this way, he became friendly with Uruguayan intellectuals - including Eduardo Galeano[32] - and collaborated in the planning and production of the *Enciclopedia Cultural Uruguaia,* directed by Angel Rama[33] .

Another significant moment was the additional opportunity for Darcy to be appointed president of the "Seminario da Reforma da Universidade do Uruguai, which resulted in his restructuring program, the Maggio Plan" (RIBEIRO, 1990, p. 137). Commenting briefly on his Uruguayan exile, Darcy pondered: "As you can see, my long exile in Uruguay, if it wasn't full of flowers, it wasn't full of thorns either" (RIBEIRO, 1997, p. 363). Thus, it can be summed up, in the words of the

[32] Cf.: RIBEIRO, 1997, p. 363.

[33] Angel Rama is a literary critic and writer from Uruguay; he also took part, together with Darcy, in the *Seminar on autonomous cultural policy for Latin America.* The relationship between the Brazilian anthropologist and the Uruguayan writer is summarized as follows: "The interlocution between the two writers, around *culture* and literature, transcends the borders of Uruguay, revealing itself through their participation in major cultural projects (Ayacucho Library); through their literary affinities (Mario de Andrade, Guimaraes Rosa, Jose Maria Arguedas, Gabriel Garcia Marquez, Jose Marti, among others) and also through the dialogue that can be established between concepts such as "mestigagem" (Darcy Ribeiro) and "transculturagao" (Angel Rama). (...) Without a doubt, Ribeiro's dialogue with Angel Rama was one of the most fruitful. Both are obligatory references in the construction and edification of Latin American cultural criticism" (COELHO, 2005, p. 181-2. Emphasis added).

anthropologist from Minas Gerais himself:

> Over the next ten years, based on my experience at the University of Brasilia and the University of Uruguay, I went around Latin America running university reform seminars and drawing up restructuring plans. This is what I did for the national universities of Venezuela and Peru, and for the creation of new universities in Algeria and Costa Rica.
> In exile I also continued my political activism, both with my Brazilian comrades, especially Jango and Brizola, and with the Latin American governments that were working hardest to break with dependence and backwardness (RIBEIRO, 1990, p. 137).

What is most significant about this period in Uruguay is that while in Brazil his work in the educational and political fields restricted any time he could devote to more intense intellectual work, on the other hand, his exile allowed him to return to academic reflections. He highlights this:

> Uruguay was a fruitful exile for me. There, in the hours that exile gave us, I studied and wrote a lot. In fact, with no family to take care of, no old friends to receive and visit, no obligations, (...) not even political activism, there was plenty of time to relax or work. The intellectual atmosphere in Uruguay and at university was very stimulating. And I had people (...) who listened patiently to my texts. The public library was also very useful, where I found all the bibliography I could wish for on Latin America.
> There I wrote the first version of *O Povo Brasileiro,* which I abandoned in order to write an explanatory theory of Brazil, essential for our history to be understood and explained. This resulted in the six volumes of my studies on the anthropology of civilization, all written or drafted there. In Uruguay, I completed *The Civilizing Process* and *The Indians and Civilization, a* book I had owed myself for many years. There too, to rest from the hard work of preparing these theoretical books, I wrote the first version of *Maira* (RIBEIRO, 1997, p. 372-3).

We can see that, distanced from his homeland and therefore unable to participate effectively in Brazilian society, he gave himself avidly to the activity of *writing.* This makes his bibliographical output, over a period of at least twelve years, astonishing[34] .

The five volumes of *Studies in* the *Anthropology of Civilization,* entitled *The Civilizing Process, The Americas and Civilization, The Dilemma of Latin America, The Brazilians: 1. Theory of Brazil,* and *The Indians and Civilization,* as a whole - with the

[34] Haydee R. Coelho, commenting on Darcy's bibliographical production during the period of his exile, says: "Exile is not reduced to the figure of the exiled/convict who purges a wandering destiny in foreign lands, always in search of a lost identity. For a large number of intellectuals, exile represented work, production, the construction of a new order, the widening of cultural boundaries, without abandoning the political and critical stance necessary to understand our existence in the world" (COELHO, 2002, p. 222).

exception of his best-known book, *The Brazilian People*[35] , the first edition of which was published in 1995 - are the main reference in Darcy Ribeiro's work for understanding his thinking about Latin America. As such, it would be possible to say that these *Studies* constitute a work *of* exile; or *a project,* in Darcy's own words, "so ambitious that only a political exile, obsessed with the tensions of proscription, would dare to write it" *(apud* MATTOS, 2007, p. 205).

3. 2 An anthropology of civilization

Darcy Ribeiro's first effort at an interpretation of Brazil, which would later be extended to the Americas, dates back to the 1950s. The initial version of a *theory of Brazil* was the result of studies coordinated by the author in the research program of the Brazilian Center for Educational Research (CBPE), part of the National Institute of Pedagogical Studies (Inep), under the presidency of Anisio Teixeira. The organization was linked to the Ministry of Education and Culture between 1957 and 1960 (PINHEIRO, 2006). CBPE's aim was to subsidize educational policies by investing in research. With Darcy Ribeiro having been given the task of directing the research by Anisio, he brought together a competent and diverse team, mainly of social scientists, who sought to understand the peculiarities of each of Brazil's regions in order to design effective educational interventions. Since then, Darcy Ribeiro has been thinking about *Brazil*, impressed by its unity in diversity. However, it was not until he was in exile that he published this work, *Teoria do Brasil (Theory of Brazil*), *and* about it he stated:

> The first version of this book, some four hundred dense pages, took shape after two years of intense work. It was no longer the synthesis I had proposed. Rather, it was the version resulting from my experiences of the tragic events in Brazil in which I had played a leading role. This was the nerve that pulsed underneath the text, the search for a historical, scientific answer, in the argument that we, the losers of the military coup, were asking ourselves. Why, once again, had the ruling class beaten us? (RIBEIRO, 1995, p. 13).

[35] However, it is worth mentioning that this book is the *driving* force behind the beginning and end of all Darcy's intellectual work (Cf.: RIBEIRO, 1995, p. 11-2). He also comments that: "With the support of the Darcy Ribeiro Foundation, a DVD was recently released on the market with a series of programs shown on TV Cultura about *The Brazilian People,* with the participation of important personalities and testimonies from Darcy himself. It is a more than conclusive testament to the projection achieved by this work" (MATTOS, 2007, p. 204).

However, Darcy was dissatisfied with the first critical reading he made of the work, and it even frightened him, as he pointed out, because his contribution, in his eyes, was insufficient. Or worse, as he put it, "it didn't answer the questions I proposed, summarized in the phrase that I have since repeated: why hasn't Brazil worked out?" (RIBEIRO, 1995, p. 13). He explains:

> Its very elaboration demonstrated the lack of an interpretative theory that would allow us to effectively understand the process of formation of the Brazilian people. In order to do this, it would be necessary to rework a series of theoretical frameworks from a Brazilian and Latin American perspective. Firstly, the theories of history, particularly the Marxist scheme of succession of economic and social forms, because the ones available were obviously inexplicable. Secondly, the classifications of the American peoples and the comparative analyses of the causes of their uneven development, which were also inadequate. Thirdly, the typologies of social classes and power structures were equally unsatisfactory. Finally, critical studies of cultures and ideologies with a view to evaluating the circumstances in which they flourish or wither and their role in the process of domination of dependent peoples (RIBEIRO, 1990[2] , p. 16).

Faced with these questions, Darcy began to re-read and revise his work, which gradually grew into books. He was bothered by the need to develop an explanatory theory of Brazil, situated in a broad human history, which led him to reflect on an innovative theory of history. Darcy Ribeiro found no explanatory possibilities in the known theories. For him, these could merely serve as "a theoretical version of European performance, but they did not explain the history of the Eastern peoples, nor the Arab world, and much less us Latin Americans" (RIBEIRO, 1995, p. 14).

In this way, Darcy Ribeiro began a revision of the theories of socio-cultural evolution, in order to properly include American societies - especially Latin American ones - in human history from an autonomous perspective, and not strictly linked to European conceptions and theoretical horizons. Darcy made it clear that his "feeling was that we lacked a general theory whose light would make us explainable in our own terms", based on our experiences in history, because "theories from other contexts were all too Eurocentric and therefore powerless to make us intelligible"; Obviously, since we don't have the same past, our present doesn't match theirs either, and so "neither does our future have a common future" (RIBEIRO, 1995, p. 13). 13).

This epistemic stance helped to develop a critique of the dominant Eurocentrism of current theories of cultural evolution. The revision of these theories would be based on autochthonous studies of American origin; not with the aim of attributing a new and inconsequential hegemony, which had previously been sustained by Europe[36] , but on the contrary, with the aim of repositioning human societies in their entirety, in a comparative line of their aspects and development processes (RIBEIRO, 1978). The book *O Processo Civilizatorio: etapas da evolucao socio-cultural (The Civilizing Process: stages of socio-cultural* evolution) is the work in which Darcy Ribeiro carries out this review of the theories of historical evolution.

This commitment and theoretical perspective took on a definite body and later became known as *Post-Colonial Studies*[37] , which refers historically to the period following the decolonization processes in Africa and Asia, especially from the mid-20th century onwards. Under the influence of post-structuralism, post-colonial studies mostly include theoretical contributions from literary and cultural studies, which emerged in the mid-1980s (BALLESTRIN, 2013). The *postcolonial,* roughly speaking, critically reviews modern epistemologies, assuming them to be political-ideological oppositions which, in practice, have *silenced* cosmologies that are no less explanatory of the world and social phenomena. What draws our attention here is the fact that we have identified several thinkers who have been called *post-colonial,* without defining themselves in this way, and who emerged "even before the institutionalization of post-colonialism as a current or school of thought" (BALLESTRIN, 2013, p. 91); this would be the case of Darcy Ribeiro. This fact is explained by Adelia Miglievich-Ribeiro when she discusses the way in which Darcy Ribeiro's thought is rescued by Walter Mignolo[38] , for example, an important intellectual engaged in *post-colonial* debates - *modernity-coloniality-decoloniality.* This is how he describes it:

> Darcy Ribeiro is a Latin American intellectual who speaks from the Third World, not as a bizarre or inferior place, but as a powerful locus of

[36] This is an important concern, "that the production of knowledge here in the tropics, (...) should not be treated as a framework for Latin American social sciences.) should not be treated as a landmark of *Latin American* social sciences, thus not incurring in the same fallacy of geopolitical reproduction of knowledge, sedimented under the aegis of Eurocentrism, which characterizes knowledge elaborated in sources other than those of the hegemonic centers and, developed and written in languages other than hegemonic ones, would constitute mere local or regional knowledge" (ROMERA, 2013, p. 88, emphasis added). See also: PORTO-GONQALVES, 2005, p. 9).

[37] The term is wide-ranging and has already had its consequences. In Latin America, at the end of the 20th century, the group called *modernity-coloniality* was born; later, *modernity-coloniality-decoloniality*, which distinguishes itself from post-colonial studies, above all because of the strong influence of English and French-speaking authors on it, inaugurating a movement to reclaim Latin American critical thinking in the light of what they call the "decolonial turn", i.e. the reclaiming of Latin America as a locus of enunciation. (Cf.: MIGLIEVICH-RIBEIRO, 201 3[2]).

[38] On this appropriation of Darcynian thought, see the book: *Local Histories/Global Projects. Coloniality, subaltern knowledges and liminal thinking;* by Walter D. Mignolo (2003).

> enunciation. It is at this point that I bring Darcy - a writer from the late 1960s/70s to the 1990s - closer to the post-colonial (or post-Western) commitment, which is gaining increasing attention in this 21st century. I do this through Walter Mignolo, one of the most prominent representatives of the *modernity-coloniality* strand who, (...) chose Darcy Ribeiro, alongside Henrique Dussel and Anibal Quijano, as his privileged interlocutor (MIGLIEVICH-RIBEIRO, 2012, p. 282-3)[39] .

But, at this point, it is by focusing on two concepts proposed by Darcy Ribeiro that we can better elucidate what interests us in this research. These are the categories of "historical updating" and "evolutionary acceleration". Their high importance and originality constitute Darcynian *Studies*, and have ethical implications, allowing Darcy, at a later date, to deal with more specific cases, such as Latin American peoples. With regard to the concept of *historical updating,* Darcy proposes:

> By *historical updating* or *historical incorporation* we mean the procedures by which these historically backward peoples are compulsorily engaged in more evolved systems. This was the case, for example , with the incorporation of autochthonous peoples subjugated by the conqueror and of African populations transferred as labor force for mines and tropical plantations in the colonial slave formations of America. The concept of actualization therefore portrays both situations of a regressive nature - from the point of view of ethnic entities that have been devastated, traumatized or destroyed - and progressive contents, as a procedure for incorporating backward peoples into more advanced socio-economic systems. The fundamental characteristic of the process of historical updating lies in its sense of reflexive modernization with a loss of autonomy and the risk of ethnic disintegration (RIBEIRO, 1978, p. 56, emphasis added).

This definition brings Darcy Ribeiro closer to the reality of Latin American nations which, according to his conception, "once freed from the condition of colonial territories of a 'mercantile-salvationist' formation, fell, through historical updating, into the condition of 'neo-colonialist areas of industrial imperialist formations'" (MATTOS, 2007, p. 234). The consequent implications are seen in the progressive increase in the means of production, or even in their ways of life, but inevitably at the cost of the "establishment of relations of dependence between the governing society and the

---

39 It's worth noting here that: "Darcy's anti-colonial thinking talks to post-colonial thinking, without confusing them, by broadening the universal. Both pay attention to the violence of colonization and its consequences in the economic and symbolic dimensions of social life. The subordination and dehumanization strategies that produced the colonized, who became 'spectators overwhelmed by inessentiality', also produced the colonizer. Fanon's *culture-as-political-struggle* authorizes the dialectical reorganization of the colonial heritage that contains the germ of a free people. Post-colonial counter-discourse and decolonization can finally reinvent the subject in their true humanity, *new men*, therefore. Darcy Ribeiro pointed out that under massacres, despoliation and intense suffering, new peoples were born in the Americas, mixed in the fusion of ethnicities" (MIGLIEVICH- RIBEIRO, 2012, p. 300. Emphasis added).

peripheral society, subject to reflex action" (RIBEIRO, 1978, p. 56); since, as producers, as well as consumers of new products or goods, they assume a dependence on the import of industrial goods.

In a different process, there is the concept of *evolutionary acceleration,* designated by Darcy as:

> indicate the direct procedures, intentional or not, of inducing progress with the preservation of the autonomy of the society that experiences it and, for this very reason, with the preservation of its ethnic figure and, sometimes, with its expansion as a *macro-ethnicity* assimilating other peoples. This is the case with societies that experience a technological revolution based on their own creativity, or on the complete and autarchic adoption of technological innovations achieved by other societies, or on both sources. We also identify as situations of evolutionary acceleration the processes of ethnic reconstitution through which societies previously overwhelmed by processes of updating rebuild their own *ethos* in order to gain political independence and regain their lost autonomy (RIBEIRO, 1978, p. 56-7. Emphasis added).

Based on this definition, it is possible to delineate that, for Darcy Ribeiro, the realities he analyzed are not stagnant; on the contrary, they are absolutely subject to change and transformation, in a revolutionary process which, as a rule, is designed to lead historically backward peoples towards a conjuncture of autonomous development. In this sense, underdevelopment is "a contingent factor, not just a stage or a 'backward' state as opposed to advanced models of society" (MATTOS, 2007, p. 135).

It is interesting to mention that with the publication of his works - including the various translations and re-editions - Darcy progressively acquired international recognition. At the beginning of the 1970s, the journal *Current Anthropology,* which, according to Darcy Ribeiro, at the time could be considered the most important and significant periodical in the field of anthropology, commissioned two works from Darcy. The first was an essay called *Configuragoes Historico- Culturais dos Povos Americanos,* which refers to his book *As Americas e a Civilización: processo de formagao e causas do desenvolvimento desigual dos povos americanos.* The second text was written as a summary of the book *The Civilizing Process: stages of socio-cultural evolution*. The aim of the publication was to introduce an innovative approach to the debate and dissemination of academic research and studies of greater relevance and pertinence, known as *CA Treatment.*

This type of debate privileged works of theoretical density and prominence to be sent to the journal, such as those written by Darcy, who, in turn, sent the texts to a group of anthropologists from various nations and with respectable notoriety. The evaluations were sent to the author so that he could write his own response and, finally, all the texts were published[40] by *Current Anthropology.* Although Darcy (1975) complained that the assessments had not been as detailed or severe as he had hoped, given the polemical nature of his work, he thanked his fellow anthropologists for their comments and, in particular, for the respectful and sympathetic attitude with which they viewed his efforts. Reading this publication, between the synthesis and the summary, as well as between the criticisms and the appropriate replies, it is possible to see the remarkable relevance of Darcyn's work.

> Thus, despite the fact that *The Civilizing Process* was written by an intellectual from the underdeveloped world, in 1978, when the work was ten years old, it already had fifteen international editions and around 160,000 copies sold. In 1997, (...) *O Processo Civilizatorio* brought a list of 26 editions of the work in countries such as Brazil, Argentina, Venezuela, Mexico, Cuba, Portugal, Italy, England, the United States and Germany, which ended up being Darcy Ribeiro's most widely read and debated book in the world. And that, together with *The Americas and Civilization,* became the main reference for Darcy Ribeiro's international academic recognition (PINHEIRO, 2006, p. 77. Emphasis added).

Despite the theoretical observations that had already been formulated and substantiated, Darcy Ribeiro was not completely satisfied. The interpretative path, in his view, was not completely exhausted, and the issues dealt with in *The Civilizing Process* were not yet sufficient to make his *continental homeland* explicable. Therefore, he had to continue his theoretical elaborations that would sufficiently allow him to continue with the initial project that moved him. With this in mind, he proposed a new, more specific approach to Latin America. And so he pointed out that

> The *[Civilization] Process* was not enough. The explanation it offers for 10,000 years of history is too broad. Its answers, necessarily generic, only give tenuous outlines of our historical performance. That's all it could offer as an alternative to the classic texts with which this subject is generally dealt with. A more credible and more explanatory conceptual scheme than those available, through the proposition of new technological revolutions as the engines of history, new civilizing processes and new socio-cultural formations. Seen in this light, our reality is treated in its most general terms, resulting in an explanatory discourse that is useful for theoretical and comparative purposes, but insufficient to account for the causality of our history.
>
> I then set off in search of more down-to-earth explanations, in more years of work. The theme I now set myself was to reconstruct the process of the formation of the American peoples, in an effort to explain the causes of their

[40] "This debate was published in volumes 11 to 14 of *Current Anthropology* in 1970" (PINHEIRO, 2006, p. 77), and later published in book form by Darcy Ribeiro (1975).

> uneven development. I thus leapt from 10,000 years of general history to 500 years of American history with a new book: *The Americas and Civilization,* in which I proposed a typology of the American peoples, in the form of a broad explanatory statement (RIBEIRO, 1995, p. 14-5).

As such, *The Americas and Civilization* consistently establishes a commitment to the anthropological interpretation of the complex social, cultural and economic factors in America that governed the formation of its national ethnicities. "Its basic objective is to analyze the causes of the uneven development of American societies" (RIBEIRO, 1983, p. 9).

These studies that make up his *anthropology of civilization* show Darcy's reformist stance, put into practice through his political action, concomitant with his theoretical work: both are inseparable. After graduating from the Free School of Sociology and Politics (ELSP) in Sao Paulo for ten years, Darcy Ribeiro devoted his scientific activity to studying the Indians and the sertanejos, when he was then "summoned" to exercise political and advisory functions in the field of Education by the man he came to call his master, Anisio Teixeira. It was Anisio who took him to CBPE-Inep and because of his prestige with Juscelino Kubitschek, having been asked to coordinate education in the new capital, Brasilia, he took the young and intrepid Darcy Ribeiro with him. Darcy took over the coordination of the work to create Brasilia's first university, the UnB, and was its first rector. Then, during Brazil's short parliamentary term, he was Joao Goulart's Minister of Education and Culture. With the return to presidentialism, he left the ministry to become Chief of Staff of the Jango government (MIGLIEVICH-RIBEIRO, 2012[2]). It was clear that these experiences, and so many other *things* he *did,* were responsible to a greater or lesser extent for the themes and objectives of his *studies.* Even so, he assumed that both his experiences, as a scientist and as an engaged politician, "explain his interest in understanding the socio-cultural processes that dynamize the lives of the American peoples", and that they "lead some of them to full development and others to backwardness" (RIBEI RO, 1983, p. 13).

It would be impossible not to notice the revolutionary character, as well as the remarkable optimism for the future, expressed in his writings, including books, articles, novels and letters, both revealed in an effort to demonstrate the means of overcoming the backwardness of *underdeveloped* nations, or, to put it another way, the mechanisms of domination and dispossession to which they are thus subjected. The clear objective of the Brazilian anthropologist was to show that there is a better future, a nobler path for all impoverished nations, especially for Brazil, his country, a future to be fully conquered by a radical transformation of the existing reality.

In order to oust a ruling class that is committed almost exclusively to its own interests, which in this case are convergent with the interests of (neo)imperialist geopolitics, and therefore antagonistic to the fate and success of its own country, a social revolution is essential, resulting from the maturation of a critical consciousness. The *revolution* is, from then on, the way for impoverished nations - Latin American and, especially, Brazilian - to emerge from this condition and take the lead in their own destiny, integrating and making themselves autonomous in world civilization. This would be Darcy's utopia, as proposed by Andre Mattos (2007). As such, the phrase that Darcy uttered to everyone who would listen, and especially to his close friends, is emblematic, as Eric Nepomuceno (2001, p. 58) recalled: "In Latin America, we only have two ways out: to be resigned, or to be indignant. And I will never resign myself.

Latin America, according to Darcy Ribeiro, is not just the result of the sum of two thousand years of Latinity, or of five centuries of European occupation. But with this historical heritage, it has been possible to acquire two continental characteristics. The first is that we are an ancient civilization, just as the Iberian cultures of which we are heirs are ancient, in full symbiosis with a second characteristic, which is that we are new peoples, expressed as ethnic groups. Darcy Ribeiro categorizes it as follows, initially, in the degradation of the old:

> The old heritage expresses itself socially in its worst aspects: the consular and alienated attitude of the ruling classes; the caudillian habits of command and the taste for personal power; the deep social discrimination between rich and poor, which separates men more than the color of their skin; the manorial customs such as the enjoyment of leisure, the cult of courtesy among patricians, the contempt for work, the conformism and resignation of the poor with their poverty (RIBEIRO, 1983, p. 86-7).

On the other hand, in the new, it is possible to find the manifestation of our virtues:

> The new is expressed in the affirmative energy that emerges from the oppressed layers, finally awakened to the profane and eradicable nature of the misery in which they have always lived; in the increasingly lucid and proud assumption of their own ethnic-mestizo image; in the equating of the causes of backwardness and penury and in the rebellion against the prevailing order (RIBEIRO, 1983, p. 87).

The collision between these two characteristics of life and society is the "Latin

American social revolution in progress", because this *revolution* will grant, in due course, "the peoples of brown America the creative impetus lost centuries ago by their Iberian matrixes, when they were late in integrating themselves into industrial civilization, thus entering into decadence" (RIBEIRO, 1983, p. 87). According to Darcy, this revolution is necessary, because it will involve Latin Americans entering into dialogue with other peoples, whatever they may be, in the category of peoples capable of contributing in a specific way to a healthy ecumenical civilization. This contribution would be the result of our own ethnic configuration, as well as their virtualities, which would culminate in making everyone "more human, because they have incorporated more racial and cultural faces of man" (RIBEIRO, 1983, p. 87).

In the book *The Americas and Civilization,* this theoretical conception constitutes the genesis for the elaboration of ethno-national typologies of extra-European peoples, which served as the foundation for practically all the texts written during the period of exile, aimed at the study and knowledge of the various socio-cultural formations in Latin America.

It is worth mentioning that Darcy also continued his research, looking for elements for a better and effective understanding of Latin American societies, starting from the cultural level, wanting them to act on the situation of dependence in relation to the geopolitical centers of power. This new research would focus on elucidating the character of underdevelopment to which Latin America has remained subject, especially with regard to its widespread dependence on North America; and analyzing the conflicts that have erupted on the continent in the midst of the power structures that want and insist on maintaining the social order in its current configuration - which continues to favor them - and clashing with the virtually insurgent forces that want and seek to transform it (RIBEIRO, 1983[2]). This need for theoretical advance is exemplified in the author's own words:

> There was still a lack of a theory of culture capable of dealing with our reality, in which erudite knowledge is so often spurious and popular non-knowledge is constantly reaching critical heights, mobilizing consciences for profound movements of social reordering. How can we establish the form and role of our erudite culture, made of transplants, governed by European fashions, in the face of popular creativity, which blends the most disparate traditions to understand this new version of the world and of ourselves? I wrote *The Dilemma of Latin America* to address this need. In it, I propose new schemes for social classes and political performances, situating them under the North American hegemonic pressure in which we exist, without being us, to be what suits them (RIBEIRO, 1995, p. 16).

Although an academic construction is evident in *The Dilemma of Latin America,* the work also makes explicit his increasing and more frequent involvement in political movements and actions in different Latin American countries, as well as the absorption of the literature he came into contact with in those countries into his writing. As Lucas Pinheiro (2006) points out, the *praxeological* process of constructing his studies modified his language; his thought and discourse acquired a more essayistic tone, and with this, he lost his "scientificity" according to the assessments of that period, which, we suppose, should not justify a disparagement of his work, on the contrary.

Darcy, in *The Americas and Civilization,* warned beforehand of his intention to "reconstruct the process of formation of the American peoples with a view to diagnosing their development problems", but that he had to observe that "in the impetuous dynamics of the political life of peoples, their destiny is defined and their potential realized", It is impossible to get away from this fact, especially for "those who study and write inspired by the desire to influence the process of change in order to help set in motion the necessary revolution" (RIBEIRO, 1983, p. 7). 7). Thus,

> Darcy Ribeiro therefore reinforced that from a certain point onwards, his intellectual stance ceased to be a "merely academic exercise" and became a "deliberate effort to contribute to an active awareness of the causes of underdevelopment" of the Latin American peoples. This would justify taking political positions which, for Darcy Ribeiro himself, meant representing the interests of certain social classes to the detriment of others: "For me, the intellectual is the one who best masters and expresses the knowledge of his group" (PINHEIRO, 2006, p. 154).

3. 3 Historical and Cultural Configurations

Darcy Ribeiro developed an original explanatory theory for Latin America, and in this he did not exclude the recognition given to European participation in the process of transfiguring the peoples who lived here. To understand the history of peoples and civilizations in recent centuries is to note that, in particular, "the history of the expansion of Western Europe, which, by becoming the nucleus of a new process of civilization, is thrown upon all peoples in successive waves of violence, greed and oppression", obviously involved the whole world, subjugating them to European domination in accordance with its interests, causing: "every people and even every human person, wherever they were born and lived, ended up being affected and engaged in the European economic system", configuring itself, "in the ideals of wealth, power, justice, or holiness inspired by it" (RIBEIRO, 1983, p. 51).

> In their expansion, the European formulas of truth, justice and beauty progressively imposed themselves as compulsory values. They were as powerful for the persuasive force of their universality as for the coercive mechanisms through which they spread. At the same time, European languages spread throughout the world, all originating from a single trunk, and were spoken by more people than any other group of languages that had previously existed. Their various cults, born of the same religion, became ecumenical. Its science and the technologies derived from it spread throughout the earth. Its artistic heritage and the multiplicity of styles in which it expresses itself become universal canons of beauty. Its family, political and legal institutions, molded and remolded according to the same premises, become the order of social life for most peoples (RIBEIRO, 1983, p. 62-3).

This same process can be seen in the case of Latin America in its civilizational configuration. Understood through historical updating, the overpowering of American societies is evident, with the aim of inserting them into the world economic system. "In this way, the indigenous Americans and also the black Africans who were brought to America leapt to a higher stage of human evolution", as part of an active mercantile formation, "but were simultaneously engaged as 'external proletariats' of the metropolitan economies" (RIBEIRO, 1983, p. 41).

Aware of European action and intervention in reconfiguring the historical and cultural reality that would come to dominate the Americas, Darcy proposes a characterization of the extra-European peoples, and more specifically, what is pertinent here, of the American peoples. He then constructively outlines a perspective of autonomous development, as opposed to historical backwardness:

> the proposed historical-cultural configurations constitute congruent categories of peoples, based on the parallelism of their historical process of ethno-national formation, the uniformity of their social characteristics and the development problems they face. It is in terms of these broad configurations of peoples - rather than the nationalities that make them up, their respective racial compositions or climatic, religious and other differentiators - that each non-European people of the modern world can be situated, in order to explain how they came to be what they are now; to understand why they have experienced such different historical processes of socio-economic development; and to determine the factors which, in each case, have acted as accelerators or retarders of their integration into the lifestyle of modern industrial societies (RIBEIRO, 1983, p. 88-9). 88-9).

In this way, Darcy Ribeiro explained a classification of the non-European peoples of the *modern world,* by means of generic and approximate designations of the different peoples he analyzed. "Each one of them encompasses populations that are very different, but also sufficiently homogeneous in terms of their basic characteristics and development problems" (RIBEIRO, 1983, p. 87), with which they were confronted, thus legitimizing each of them as distinct categories. He called this *classification Historical-Cultural Configurations.* These ethno-national typologies are named as follows: the *Witness Peoples,* the *New Peoples,* the *Transplanted Peoples* and the *Emerging Peoples,* which we will briefly outline here.

The first group, which Darcy called the *Testimonial Peoples,* correspond to those who are "the modern representatives of old civilizations", who were devastated by the "traumatizing impact of European expansion, from which they are now beginning to recover from the most precarious conditions of impoverishment" (RIBEIRO, 1983, p. 539). This group can be exemplified by the Muslims, Indians, Koreans, Indochinese, Aztecs and Incas; with only Japan and China singled out by Darcy as those who, "have managed to achieve modern industrial development, the former more mature, but the latter with much greater economic potential for consolidation and expansion" (RIBEIRO, 1983, p. 539). In other words,

> We call Mexican, Meso-American and Andean populations *Witness Peoples*, as survivors of ancient civilizations - Aztec, Mayan and Inca - that collapsed under the impact of European expansion, entering a secular process of acculturation and ethnic reconstitution, which is still unfinished for all of them. (...) Paralyzed by the Spanish attack, Mexican, Mayan and Incan society collapsed; their ruling classes were replaced by foreign minorities who, from then on, began to reshape their cultures through all sorts of compulsions. This designation was carried out through various mechanisms, including the intentional decimation of the former governmental and priestly class, which was the custodian of the erudite tradition of those cultures; and the depopulation caused, subsequently, by the epidemics with which they were infected, by the engagement of slave labor and by the effect of technical and agricultural innovations that unbalanced their former subsistence system, altering their ecological base. (...) For decades, the *Witness Peoples of* America have not had their own defined and congruent way of life. The old had died as an integrating force and a new one had not yet emerged. Worn down by epidemics, driven to despair by slavery, they became herds, whose members were born and died, only living to fulfill the fate imposed on them. Throughout all this time, however, they preserved and passed on, from generation to generation, scraps of old values whose actualization in conduct was impossible but which still moved their descendants (RIBEIRO, 1983, p. 108-9).

Another *historico-cultural configuration* is formed by the *Transplanted Peoples,* which are the result of the migration of large population contingents, mostly Europeans, to, among other regions, especially the Americas, with the intention of rebuilding their own conceptions of life in new geographies. "Each of them structured themselves according to the models of economic and social life of the nation from which they came, carrying forward, in their adopted lands, processes of renewal that were already operating in the old European contexts" (RIBEIRO, 1975, p. 43).

These *Transplanted Peoples* differ from the other *historical and cultural configurations* by their characteristically European aspect, expressed even phenotypically, found in their predominantly Caucasoid form, and as Darcy explained, "in the ideological profile and also in the more maturely capitalist character of their economy" (RIBEIRO, 1975, p. 43); and he adds that such a configuration,

> is based mainly on modern industrial technology and the integrating capacity of its social structure, which has incorporated almost all of its population into the productive system and most of it into the social, political and cultural life of the nation. For this very reason, they face different national and social problems and have a different view of the world from the American peoples of other categories (RIBEIRO, 1975, p. 43).

For example, taking a broader approach, Australia and New Zealand are *Transplanted Peoples,* as are Israel, the South African Union and Rhodesia, within their respective neo-European specificities. In the American territory, the United States and Canada in the north are designated as such, while in the south, Uruguay and Argentina are emblematic.

Although it is possible to identify the United States and Canada, on the one hand, and Uruguay and Argentina, on the other, as participants in the same bloc of *Transplanted Peoples,* because they belong to the same European derivation, Darcy points out that there are other differentiating and approximating criteria:

> In the first cases, we come across nations resulting from colonization projects set up in territories whose tribal populations were decimated or confined to *reservations* so that a new society could settle in them. In the case of the people of Rio Plata, we find the result of a peculiar undertaking by a Creole elite - entirely alienated from and hostile to its own ethnic *group* of *Pueblo Nuevo* - which adopted as a national project the replacement of its own people by white, swarthy Europeans, conceived as people with a greater vocation for progress. Argentina and Uruguay are thus the result of a process of ecological succession deliberately triggered by the national oligarchies, through which a *New-People* configuration is transformed into a *Transplanted-People.* In this process, the *Ladin* and *Gaucho* population, *which* originated from the mestipation of the Iberian settlers with the indigenous, was crushed and replaced as the basic contingent of the nation by a number of European immigrants (RIBEIRO, 1975, p. 44).

Therefore, even though he places all these ethnic groups in the same category of *Transplanted Peoples,* Darcy specifies the existence and need for differentiators:

> Between the *transplanted peoples,* especially those in the north and south of the continent, there are profound differences, resulting not only from cultural matrices, predominantly Latin and Catholic in one case, Anglo-Saxon and Protestant in the other, but also from the degree of development. These discrepancies bring Argentinians and Uruguayans closer together and identify them with the other Latin American peoples, who are also neo-Latin, also Catholic and also poor and backward. For most of their other characteristics, however, they are *Transplanted Peoples* and, as such, share many common traits with the colonizers of the North (RIBEIRO, 1983, p. 414-5).

Another category is that of *New Peoples,* "which undoubtedly occupies the greatest space in Darcy's discussions, above all because Brazil is included among them" (MATTOS, 2007, p. 240). This *historical and cultural configuration* comes from the combination, deculturization and melding of disparate ethnic matrices such as the indigenous, African and European. This is how it is explained:

> The *Povos-Novos* were formed by the confluence of deeply disparate racial, cultural and linguistic contingents, as a by-product of European colonial projects. By bringing together blacks, whites and Indians to open up large plantations of tropical products or for mining, with the sole aim of serving European markets and generating profits, the colonizing nations ended up shaping peoples who were profoundly different from themselves and from all the other formative matrices.
>
> When confronted in the same communities, these basic contingents, although playing different roles, began to mix and fuse culturally to a greater extent than in any other type of conjuncture (RIBEIRO, 1983, p. 92).

According to Darcy, the *Povos-Novos* constitute the most representative *historical and cultural configuration of* the Americas, as they permeate the entire continent, in the most varied porpositions, exemplified by Brazil, Paraguay, Venezuela, Colombia and Chile, as well as the Antilleans and part of Central and South America in the United States (RIBEIRO, 1975). This designation, therefore, is expressed in consonance with a fundamental configuration of *"especia novae,* as ethnic entities distinct from their formative matrices", as well as because it representatively anticipates what will still "probably be the human groups of the distant future: increasingly mestipated and uniformed and, in this way, racially and culturally homogenized" (RIBEIRO, 1975, p. 27).

What is most significant here is what stimulates the approximation and differentiation of all the *New Peoples* within this designation. In other words, the elementary and defining characteristic of their *historical and cultural configuration* is, in particular, the form of action taken by the Europeans in their intermingling with Africans and Indians; concomitant with the type of society that generally took shape between them:

> We come across the emergence of New Peoples through the combination and amalgamation of originally very different ethnic groups, under conditions of despotic domination by colonial agents from more developed societies or by *herenvolkers* capable of conquering and dynamizing societies immersed in feldalism and integrating them into imperial bodies and international mercantile systems (...). The *New Peoples of* the Americas are also the result of specific forms of domination and productive organization under conditions of extreme social oppression and compulsory culture which, although exercised at other times and in different areas of the world, reached the widest and most rigorous application in colonial America. These were, firstly, the European colonization of the New World, through slavery used as a capitalist-mercantile process to recruit the labour of tribal peoples, Africans and Aborigines, for agricultural production and mineral exploitation. Secondly, the establishment of the *hacienda* as a basic social institution and as a model of capitalist business organization which, by combining the domination of the land and the monopoly of the labour force, made it possible to produce articles for the world market, in order to obtain pecuniary profits (RIBEIRO, 1983, p. 206-7. Emphasis added).

The common, fundamental aspects of the *historical and cultural configurations of* all the nations and enclaves that designate them as *New Peoples are* not only expressed in a formative process. It is revealed simultaneously in their profiles and problems of ethno-national maturation, as well as in their socio-economic development.

In general terms, and from a politico-social point of view, the colonial slave enterprises in the Americas, the new population, born and integrated in the plantations and mines, "was no longer European, nor African, nor indigenous, but configured protocells of a new ethnic body" (RIBEIRO, 1975, p. 29). In summary, it is possible to specify the *Povos-Novos* as follows:

> All located in Latin America, they are divided into three large blocs. Firstly, the 120 million Chileans, Brazilians and Paraguayans, who together form the most populous group. The first two have advanced and diversified industrialization, which guarantees them certain conditions for independent development. But they do so with different ends and means. Brazil and Paraguay, dominated by military autocracies, seek the prosperity of large companies, predominantly foreign, and of a narrow ruling class that concentrates power and wealth. Chile, oriented between 1970 and 1973 towards an evolutionary socialism, sought to achieve generalizable progress for the entire population within a multi-party parliamentary regime, but was defeated. Secondly, the peoples of New Granada, made up of Colombia, Venezuela and the Guianas, whose economies have been profoundly deformed by the intervention of the big US monopoly corporations and by the hegemony of the old ruling classes made up of bosses - oligarchs, bosses - parastatals and bosses - bureaucrats, who are all working together to perpetuate backwardness and thus safeguard their minority interests. The basic problem facing all these countries is to emancipate themselves from this dual domination in order to achieve development. Thirdly, the 23 million

> Antilleans, who are also polarized between two models of economic and social order: the Cuban socialist model and the US imperialist model, but who are forbidden by the latter's veto from deliberating on the path that best suits their people (RIBEIRO, 1983, p. 540-1).

Finally, another category that is proposed among the *historical-cultural configurations* is that of *Emergent Peoples,* "which receives little attention from Darcy compared to the others" (MATTOS, 2007, p. 240). These are represented by nations "that emerge from tribal to national conditions" (RIBEIRO, 1983, p. 539), corresponding to the nations that emerged in Africa and Asia during the processes of decolonization, and which made an ascendancy from the tribal level or from a condition of mere colonial trading posts to national societies that claim to be autonomous. What characterizes them is the fact that, despite their "situation of even greater backwardness than that faced by Latin American nations at the time of their Independence in the first quarter of the last century", according to Darcy, they would have "possibilities of a more accelerated and less dependent development, due to the world situation divided by the opposition between the socialist and capitalist camps" (RIBEIRO, 1983, p. 539). Darcy Ribeiro identifies the development of resistance as "differentiating energies that promise to preserve, for the world of the future, multiple unique ethnic faces" (RIBEIRO, 1975, p. 52), and although he does not explain why some ethno-racial manifestations are due, he also extends their existence to Latin America:

> A quick examination of the situation of Latin America's indigenous populations shows that most of them have disappeared into the *Pueblos Nuevos* or the *Pueblos Transplantandos*, or only survive as small, marginalized ethnic enclaves in the face of the mass national population. Their fate, whatever it may be, will not affect the national destiny. Even so, in these cases there are some exceptions; that is, tribal peoples who will resist long enough to survive and grow as an ethnic face of their own in the future. This will happen, for example, with the *Mapuche* (700,000), who currently represent 7% of the Chilean population, but who are growing at such an intense rate that they are likely to double and triple their proportion within the total population of Chile in the coming decades. As this growth is taking place among a people who are aware of their individuality, bitter about the secular oppression they have suffered and continue to suffer, and who are demanding their rights, it is to be expected that the interethnic tensions that have so often convulsed the south of Chile will once again be activated. The same tends to occur, albeit within a less tense framework, with other indigenous groups that have relatively large populations, such as the *Cuna* of Panama (200,000), the *Guajiro* (100,000) on the Venezuelan-Colombian borders and the *Chiriguano* (70,000) of Paraguay (RIBEIRO, 1975, p. 54-5. Emphasis added).

And with this, he adds that,

> In all these cases, we are dealing with populations from pre-Columbian tribal indigenous ethnic groups who, despite experiencing the impact of civilization over the centuries, have managed to maintain a sizeable population nucleus. Their situation is therefore different from the numerous tribal micro-ethnicities that have managed to survive - in the Amazon, for example - because they have distanced themselves from the frontiers of civilization, avoiding contact with its lethal effects. The cases mentioned are different because they are peoples who have suffered all the deleterious effects of the impact with civilization and yet have resisted, grown and rebuilt their *ethos*. Now they aspire to re-emerge from the future, as Emergent Peoples or as components of new multi-national units that recognize their right to be themselves (RIBEIRO, 1975, p. 55. Emphasis added).

3. 4 Latin American identity

In order to substantiate the aspects that would contribute to the formation of a unique Latin American identity, Darcy Ribeiro analyzes the issues that would lead to achieving this project. He points to geographical barriers as a preliminary problem to be overcome. In his attempt to elucidate the meaning of Latin America's existence, he designates it as "the fruit of its continental continuity", although he clarifies the fact that "geographical unity has never functioned here as a unifying factor because the different colonial implementations from which Latin American societies were born coexisted", since "each one of them was directly related to the colonial metropole" (RIBEIRO, 1986, p.
11). And he adds that Latin American nations are still focusing on foreign world economic centers, disregarding the potential of the continent nearby.

Another difficulty pointed out by Darcy is on the linguistic-cultural level, which is also an inhomogeneous category. Reducing the scale from Latinos to Iberians could result in a subtly more uniform unity, but with little legitimacy, "because it would exclude only the descendants of French colonization"; however, by reducing the referential scale of analysis from an Iberian perspective into two distinguishable categories, we would have: "A Luso-American content concentrated entirely in Brazil and a Hispano-American content that brings together the rest", which would obviously present minor differences, "because it is based on a small linguistic variation that is not enough to be an obstacle to communication", even if, "we tend to exaggerate it on the basis of a long common history, interacting but often conflicting" (RIBEIRO, 1986, p. 12). 12).

Pointing out the similarities and differences between Latin Americans, he points out the importance of indigenous people in the ethnic composition of countries like Guatemala and the Andean Altiplano, where this presence is more noticeable, constituting an ethno-cultural unity, or even in Mexico, where an enormous number of indigenous people predominate in certain regions - as well as in other countries, Bolivia, Peru, Ecuador and Colombia, for example - and he projects with a certain enthusiasm that "in the next few years, profound social upheavals of a national nature will take place in these places, or they will be restructured as federations of autonomous peoples" (RIBEIRO, 1986, p. 13). 13). As for the other countries, he adds:

> The situation in other countries, where only tribal micro-ethnicities can be found, immersed in vast ethnically homogeneous national societies, is totally different. (...) All these peoples have one of their genetic and cultural matrices in the Aborigine, but his contribution has been absorbed to such an extent that whatever the fate of the surviving indigenous populations, their ethnic configuration will not change much. In other words: the miscegenation, absorption and Europeanization of the former indigenous groups within the national population is complete or underway anc tends to homogenize - although not merge - all the ethnic matrices, converting them into different ways of participating in the same national ethnicity This does not mean that the Indians who survived as tribes in these countr es will disappear. On the contrary, despite being increasingly acculturated, they will survive differentiated and will be ever more numerous (RIBEIRO, 1986, p. 13-4).

Alongside the indigenous, another matrix, which, in addition to the European element, has a third reference, is the black African. This massively permeates the Brazilian coast, and various other areas throughout Latin America. In addition, it is antagonistic to any differences announced by anthropologists, who, excessively or not, have elaborated cultural continuities in an attempt to highlight these *nuclei*'s links to their cultural matrices; Darcy, however, asserts "that, here too, the similarities are more significant than the differences, since all these contingents are fully 'Americanized'" (RIBEIRO, 1986, p. 15). It is true that these three matrices, placed from the point of view of miscegenation, and therefore together, express a fundamental reference for the reinvention and ethno-cultural vindication of Latin American peoples. This shows that it is fallacious to suggest a predominance of Iberian culture in defining Latin American identity; on the contrary, the idea of a multicultural, mestizo and hybrid civilization is based on mestigagem. In this way, Darcy argues in favor of a "uniformity without unity":

> Above the crossed lines of so many differentiating factors - the origin of the colonizer, the presence or absence and weight of the indigenous and African contingent and other components - what stands out in the Latin American

> world is the unity of the product resulting from the Iberian expansion over America and its successful process of homogenization. With all these contingents - present to a greater or lesser extent in one region or another - ethno-national societies have been built whose populations are the product of crossbreeding and want to continue merging. (...)(...) By bringing together people from all over the world, new mestigos have been created here who bear in their ethno-cultural faces heritages taken from all the matrices of humanity. (...) What stands out as explanatory is therefore, once again, the uniformity and the process of homogenization that encompasses more than 90% of Latin Americans. This same ongoing homogenization is notorious on certain levels, such as linguistic and cultural. (...) In fact, the Castilian and Portuguese spoken in the Americas have experienced fewer regional variations than in their countries of origin. (...).In other words: the Spanish, Portuguese and English, who had never managed to assimilate the linguistic-dialectal pockets of their small territories, when they moved to the Americas imposed on their immensely larger colonies an almost absolute linguistic uniformity and an equally remarkable cultural homogeneity (RIBEIRO, 1986, p. 17-8).

Darcy doesn't mind if such uniformity is not yet clearly perceived in all national entities, not least because, according to the anthropologist, each nationality also strives to highlight singularities as a means of self-affirmation; a stance which makes sense to those who share these same ethnic loyalties and are not incompatible with the Latin American sentiment built up in the history of the "new peoples". In the constitution of Latin American identity, as Darcy claims, the perception of ancestral peoples is evident, as well as those from other continents, which is why he sees in Latin America an "essential macroethnic identity" capable of unfolding into "a federation of Latin American national states". Darcy puts this in terms of a historical impossibility, because "Bolivar's goal was to oppose the northern United States to the southern United States"; likewise, "Artigas' Patria Grande, Marti's *Nuestra America* point in the same direction" (RIBEIRO, 1986, p. 19. Emphasis added). More viscerally, Darcy Ribeiro sees Brazilians as belonging to the geopolitical and cultural entity called Latin America.

This recurring project, which in Darcy Ribeiro would be found as a special and utopian motivation, emerges as an undeniable and irreducible contradiction between the previous purpose of the colonizer (and his heirs) and the interests of a human community resulting from this colonizing process. In other words, the opposition is explicit "between the purposes and procedures of the dominant, subordinate class, and the majority of the population that activated the enterprise, first colonial, then national" (RIBEIRO, 1986, p. 21):

> For this population, the challenge posed over the centuries was to mature as a people for themselves, aware of their interests, aspiring to co-participate in

> commanding their own destiny. Given the class opposition, it was a question of achieving these goals through the struggle against the managerial ruling class of the old social order. Even today, this is the main challenge facing all of us in Latin America (RIBEIRO, 1986, p. 21).

In this way, the utopia of a *Latin American nation,* outlined by Darcy Ribeiro, becomes increasingly evident: "Latin America has always existed under the sign of utopia. I am even convinced that utopia has its place. And here" (RIBEIRO, 1986, p. 65). In this way, he tries to signal that what Christianity achieved in American lands as its utopia, a utopia alien to the Latin American people, now forms the opposite project, meaning a break with the European "utopian" perspective: "A singular characteristic of Latin America is its condition as a group of peoples intentionally constituted by acts and wills alien to themselves" (RIBEIRO, 1986, p. 77). Antagonistic to this common condition of exploitation, Darcy points out the need for Latin Americans to unite as a people who,

> The desire to have the right job, to eat every day, to have a complete primary education, to be treated for serious illnesses and to retire at the age of seventy, are so far beyond the system's possibilities that many people can no longer sleep. There is no possibility, even in the most distant horizons of Latin America's development as it is now on the road to underdevelopment, of realizing this simple utopia in any foreseeable time (RIBEIRO, 1986, p. 70).

Darcy Ribeiro radicalizes, without any fear or temerity, the expectations he had for Latin America, both in terms of its role and autonomous development, and in terms of what it would have to do vis-à-vis other nations and continents:

> It's high time we washed the eyes of the world to teach it to see us for who we are, without hiding behind stereotypes. The idea of a Latin America of *siesta* and *fiesta,* of machismo, of vocational dictators, of shade and fresh water and of an unhealthy indolence, has the same function as racism. It is to conceal the reality of colonial and class domination (RIBEIRO, 1986, p. 101). Imagine with me, reader, that in the year 2000, Latin America will be worth fifty Cubas of power and determination as a warm presence in a world in need of daring liberation. It's not even impossible for the Third World to become the First. (...) Get used to the idea, reader, that we're going to succeed and that it won't do the world much good. We are and see ourselves as part of Western civilization. Alternates of Eastern civilizations such as India, China and Japan. But we are well aware that we are a suburb of it, more distant and differentiated from its proud central nuclei than the Soviets, as well as being immensely less important. We still have little or no awareness of the fact that the task of creating a new Westernity that is, for the first time, a respectable human civilization will fall largely on our shoulders. In the meantime, in the face of Saxon America's infectious hegemony, which seems only concerned with making a profit and holding history still; in the face of a Europe reduced to its geographical expression, divided by the arbitrary border lines of the two great hegemonic powers and

> cowering in fear of the third war that will break out on the eve of its destruction; faced with a socialist world prevented from realizing its liberating potential, overwhelmed as it is by the task of maintaining the power of reprisal with an economy five times smaller than that of its adversaries; faced with all this, I can only see us for the urgent task of humanizing our civilization and guiding it along paths of solidarity that will free men from fear and give them back the joy of living (RIBEIRO, 1986, p. 105-6). 105-6).

This utopia, according to Darcy Ribeiro, imposes itself on Latin America as responsible for redefining and effectively remaking the human civilizational path, through its emergent character, liquidating a historical legacy of suffering and exploitation that has underpinned its trajectory. This would be the *necessary revolution,* through which Latin Americans would flourish in the brilliance of their multicolored people, just like the landscape of this very land, in the certainty of fulfilling their destiny:

> Our destiny is to unify with all Latin Americans by our common opposition to the same antagonist, which is Anglo-Saxon America, in order to found, as is happening in the European community, the Latin American Napoleon dreamed of by Bolivar. Today there are 500 million of us, tomorrow there will be 1 billion. In other words, a human contingent large enough to embody Latinity in the face of the Chinese, Slavic, Arab and Neo-British blocs in future humanity. We are peoples still struggling to make ourselves a new human race that has never existed before. (...) It [Japan] now needs to master the technology of the future civilization in order to become an economic power with self-sustaining progress. We are building ourselves in the struggle to flourish tomorrow as a new civilization, mestizo and tropical, proud of itself. Happier, because it suffers more. Better, because it incorporates more humanities. More generous, because it is open to coexistence with all races and cultures and because it is based in the most beautiful and luminous province on Earth (RIBEIRO, 1995, p. 454-5).

FINAL CONSIDERATIONS

On the TV program *Sempre um Papo*[41] , which aired on June 15, 2009 to commemorate Leonardo Boff's 70th birthday[42] , we found a very interesting interview with this Brazilian theologian and philosopher. The programme was hosted by writer and cultural producer Afonso Borges and Juarez Guimaraes, organizer of the book *Leituras Criticas sobre Leonardo Boff.* Commenting on the same book, which provides a critical reflection on his work, Boff humbly assumed that he had limitations as an intellectual, and not only that, but that he saw himself as Karl Marx, in other words, *as a dwarf on the shoulders of giants.* He then mentions what he believes to be one of the best examples of these *giants* who helped him to go beyond the obvious, in his words:

> I had the opportunity to meet important people in our country, and one of them who left a deep impression on me was Darcy Ribeiro. I consider him to be one of the most intelligent people I have met in my life. I've travelled a lot, to many places in the world, attended many universities and spoken to people who are recognized all over the world for their contribution to creativity and thought. But Darcy Ribeiro was a volcano, indomitable, in language words couldn't describe his thought, and I learned a lot from him, especially this deep love for the Brazilian people, and the dream he had that we, Brazil, are the Tropical Rome - well, a bit big [*sic.*] - but a Rome not of imperialism, not of armies, but the Rome of cordiality, of the enchanted vision of the world, of this miscegenation of all ethnicities and peoples, creating an extraordinary synthesis (BOFF, 2009).

Boff's comment on the person and work of Darcy is emblematic. Especially considering that the Brazilian theologian himself is considered one of the greatest

---

[41] It is a cultural program broadcast on *TV Camara,* a public television network that primarily broadcasts news, discussions and votes from the plenary and government committees. The program *Sempre um Papo (Always a Chat*) is shown every two weeks and is designed to present debates with Brazilian writers, in order to provide a meeting, putting author and reader "face to face".

[42] Leonardo Boff is Brazilian and was born in Concordia-SC on December 14, 1938. He is considered one of the greatest exponents of *Liberation Theology* in Brazil and Latin America. He was a member of the Order of Friars Minor, also known as *Franciscans.* He became known worldwide, especially for his history of defending social causes and, more recently, in debates on environmental issues. He was ordained a priest in 1964 and in 1970 he received a doctorate in philosophy and theology from the University of Munich in Germany. He taught Systematic and Ecumenical Theology at the Franciscan Theological Institute in Petropolis, Rio de Janeiro, for 22 years. He has taught philosophy, theology, ecology and spirituality at various academic institutes in Brazil and abroad. As a visiting professor, he has taught at the following institutions: University of Lisbon (Portugal); University of Salamanca (Spain); Harvard University (United States); University of Basel (Switzerland); University of Heidelberg (Germany); among others. He holds an *Honorary Doctorate* in Politics from the University of Heidelberg (Germany); in Theology from the University of Lund (Sweden), and from the Faculty of the Escola Superior de Teologia-EST, in Sao Leopoldo-RS (Brazil). He is the author of 89 published works, with several translations into different languages. He has also received several awards and honors from various parts of the world for his publications. He is currently considered the most widely read Latin American theologian and philosopher in the world.

intellectuals Latin America has ever produced. In other words, his statement that Darcy was "one of the most intelligent people" he had met in his life expresses in itself the significance and scope of the work and theses of the anthropologist from Minas Gerais. It is possible to assimilate Darcy Ribeiro's innovation and perspicacity in his analysis. His theories are not the product of bookish activity; and it's not that Darcy didn't care about reading, on the contrary, he read and read a lot, works from the most varied genres, from academic titles to novels and poetry.

However, its importance and implications lie in the originality with which it critically observes the Latin American continent, and Brazil in particular, doing so in its own way. His interpretation of the Americas does not follow the version of the foreigner, the colonizer, the hegemonic Westerner. He interprets Latin America from his own experience and reality, in line with the references that were prominent here before him, from which he also learned and which pushed him forward: such as the aforementioned Simon Bolivar, Jose Marti, Manoel Bomfim, or Gilberto Freyre.

Darcy Ribeiro's perspective is based on a critical review of evolutionary theory, since, according to him, the process of ethnic formation in Latin America, and in Brazil in particular, was configured in a unique way. This process by which humanity is transformed and configured as ethnic groups and peoples is the result of socio-cultural evolution in exchange with the natural environment.

With this, his effort, as he has already summarized, came after realizing that there were no theoretical categories available to classify, or even explain, the degree of evolution of Latin American peoples, since, the usual typologies of the time did not provide sufficient conditions to cover the whole range of variations that lie at the root of the process of the formation of Latin America, since it includes everything from collecting tribes to high and sophisticated civilizations, all of which have their own cultures and are unique expressions. The differentiating issue that we see here in Darcy, which is also responsible for sustaining his recognized and praised intellectual brilliance, is his proposal to reformulate the conceptions of sociocultural evolution to serve as a basis for studies on the process of ethnic formation.

After such a critical review of evolutionary theory, based on studies recognized as *classic of* socio-cultural evolution, he satisfactorily elaborated a new schema of human development, aiming at a guiding study of the formation of the American peoples. In doing so, he presented the causes of the unequal development of these same peoples in a precise manner, according to what he defined as his goal.

And not only that, which in itself is no small feat. But Darcy was not satisfied. What Boff (2009) had mentioned, what impressed him most about this anthropologist, in particular, he highlighted, "this deep love for the Brazilian people and the dream he had that we, Brazil, are Tropical Rome". In other words, in Darcy we find the full symbiosis between the shrewd theoretician and the passionate utopian activist: "like few others, he combined intellectual and political work in the strict sense" (MATTOS, 2007, p. 3).

> Darcy Ribeiro's stance when writing his works is that of an observer who compares and interprets with his gaze directed at the transition from what was to what could be, attentive to the place and position from which he sees reality. He writes with the awareness of the threat hanging over Latin American countries of falling back into the condition of exploited peoples, since he admits that this is the project of the ruling classes (VAZ E SILVA, 2009, p. 24).

Darcy Ribeiro placed himself not only as the one who investigates in order to achieve a scientific verification of reality - that wouldn't be enough - but he tried, both through scientific rigor and the essayistic task, to fulfill the responsibility that he believed the intellectual had with respect to the context in which he lived. His anthropological, or even theoretical, perspective is committed to the human and placed at the service of the peoples he focuses on; which in this case refers to Latin America, and in particular - I must stress - the Brazilian people: "Throughout his life, he advocated a dark socialism that would have profound repercussions on the Brazilian soul. The formation and future of Brazil were his goal" (SANTOS and FERRAZ, 2014, p. 326).

It remains to be seen, therefore, that if Anisio Teixeira was correct, and if we have the impression that Darcy Ribeiro agreed with his master when he reaffirmed his words that "let us anticipate from Gilberto [Freyre] the greatness that the future will recognize in him, *because we all become more Brazilian with his work"* (RIBEIRO, 1997[3] , p. 8. So, our concluding hypothesis, which we are trying to corroborate here, is that we recognize the importance and significance of Darcy Ribeiro's efforts to "set in motion the *necessary revolution"* (RIBEIRO, 1983, p. 7. Emphasis added) in *Nuestra America;* and this time, with Darcy Ribeiro, at the same time, *we all become more Latin American with his work.*

In other words, we have chosen Darcy Ribeiro as one of the most significant and relevant authors for understanding and interpreting the socio-culture of Latin

America. Firstly, for demonstrating and legitimizing the ethno-cultural composition of the American peoples. And secondly, for consistently putting on the agenda a guiding and autonomous project of unity and composition of a Latin American identity, which would be feasible and realistic for all the citizens of this *Patria Grande* (RIBEIRO, 1986).

REFERENCES

AGUIAR, Ronaldo C. "An admirable book". In: BOMFIM, M. *O Brasil Nagao:* realidade da soberania nacional. Rio de Janeiro: Topbooks, 1996. pp. 22-34.

. *The forgotten rebel:* time, life and work of Manoel Bomfim. Rio de Janeiro: Topbooks, 2000.

AMARAL, Azevedo. "Prefacio a 2ª Edipao". In: BOMFIM, Manoel. *Latin America:* evils of origin. Rio de Janeiro: Topbooks, 2005. pp. 31-34.

ANDRADE, Oswald de. *A utopia antropofagica:* anthropophagy within everyone's reach. Sao Paulo: Globo, 1990.

ARAUJO, Ricardo B. de. "Chuvas de verao: 'antagonismos em equilibrio' e m Casa-Grande & Senzala de Gilberto Freyre". In: BOTELHO, A.; SCHWARCZ, L. M. (Orgs.). *An enigma called Brazil:* 29 interpreters and one country. Sao Paulo: Companhia das Letras, 2009. pp. 198-211.

ASSMANN, Hugo. *Reenchanting Education:* towards a learning society. Petropolis: Vozes, 1998.

BALLESTRIN, Luciana. "Latin America and the decolonial turn". *Brazilian Journal of Political Science.* Brasilia, May-August 2013, n° 11, pp. 89-117.

BECHELLI, Ricardo S. *Anti-racist nationalisms:* Manoel Bomfim and Manuel Gonzalez Prada. Sao Paulo: LCTE Editora, 2009.

BELLOTTO, Manoel L.; CORREA, Anna M. M. (eds). *Bolivar.* Politica - Colepao Grandes Cientistas Sociais, n° 40. Sao Paulo: Atica, 1983.

BOFF, Leonardo. "Leonardo Boff celebrates his 70th birthday". *Sempre um Papo.* TV program, duration: 54h09. General direction: Afonso Borges; Executive coordination: Ray Ribeiro. June 2009. [Available at: http://www.sempreumpapo.com.br/audiovideo/player.php?id=189. Accessed on: 05/12/2010 - 15h28].

BOLIVAR, Simon. "Letter from Jamaica". In: ZEA, L. (Compiler). *Fuentes de la cultura Latinoamericana.* Tome I. Mexico: Fondo de Cultura Economica, 1993. Pp. 17-32.

. "Angostura's Speech". In: ZEA, L. (Compiler). *Fuentes de la cultura Latinoamericana.* Tome I. Mexico: Fondo de Cultura Economica 1993². Pp. 439-460.

BOMENY, Helena. *Darcy Ribeiro:* sociology of an undisciplined man. Belo Horizonte: UFMG, 2001.

BOMFIM, Manoel. *Latin America*: evils of origin. Rio de Janeiro: Topbooks, 2005.

. *Brazil in America:* characterization of Brazilian formation. Rio de Janeiro: Topbooks, 1997.

BRAGA-PINTO, Cesar. "Gilberto Freyre's 'deviations'". *New Studies. - CEBRAP.* 2006, n.76, pp. 281-288.

BRUCE, Mariana. "Presentation". Dossie Nuestra America. *Magazine Contemporanee.* Rio de Janeiro, 2012, Year 2, n° 2, p.1-5.

BURKE, Peter. "Gilberto Freyre and the new history". *Tempo Social.* Sao Paulo, USP (SP) 1997, vol.9, n.2, pp. 1-12.

CANCLINI, Nestor G. *Latino-americanos a procura de um lugar neste seculo.* Sao Paulo: Iluminuras, 2008.

CANDIDO, Antonio. "Radicalism". *Estudos Avanqados.* Sao Paulo, vol. 4, n° 8, pp. 4-18, 1990.

CARVALHO, Eugenio R. de. "A confrontation between Norbert Elias and the Americanist ideas of Jose Marti". In: ALMEIDA, J. de. (org.) *Caminhos da historia da America no Brasil:* tendencias e contornos de um campo historiografico. Brasilia: ANPHLAC, 1998. P. 65-77.

COELHO, Claudio M. *Gilberto Freyre: indiciarismo, emoqao e politica na Casa-Grande e na Senzala.* Vitoria: Master's dissertation in History, UFES, 2007.

COELHO, Haydee R. "Culture from the perspective of Darcy Ribeiro and Angel Rama". *Via Atlantica,* n° 8, December 2005. pp. 164-183.

. "Darcy Ribeiro: the indigenous question, literary representation and its multiple interfaces". *O Eixo e a Roda: Revista de Literatura Brasileira,* vol. 21, n° 2, Belo Horizonte (MG) UFMG, 2012. pp. 161-177.

. "Listening to texts: looks at culture and identity". *Via Atlantica.* USP. Sao Paulo (SP), n° 4, 2000. pp. 140-147.

. "Darcy Ribeiro's Exile in Uruguay". *Aletria: Revista de Estudos de Literatura,* v 6, Belo Horizonte: POSLIT/CEL, Faculdade de Letras da UFMG, 2002. pp. 211-225.

DIETRICH, Wolfram. *Simao Bolivar and the Latin American wars of independence.* Porto Alegre: Edigoes Globo, 1937.

DORATIOTO, Francisco. *National spaces in Latin America:* from Bolivarian utopia to fragmentation. Sao Paulo: Brasiliense, 1994.

DUSSEL, Enrique. "Preface. In: ZIMMERMANN, R. *América Latina o Nao Ser.* uma abordagem filosofica a partir de Enrique Dussel (1962-1976). Petropolis: Vozes, 1986. pp. 13-15.

FERNANDES, Florestan. "The relevance of Jose Marti". *Opinion.* Sao Paulo, Folha de Sao Paulo newspaper, May 1995. [Available at: http://www1.folha.uol.com.br/fsp/1995/5/22/opiniao/7.html. Accessed on: 02/04/2014].

FERNANDES, Paula R. "America Latina aos olhos de Manoel Bomfim: analise da obra 'A America Latina: males de origem'". *Dimensoes.* Revista de Historia da UFES.

UFES. Vitoria (ES), vol. 29, pp. 100-118, 2012.

FONSECA, Edson N. da. *Around Gilberto Freyre:* essays and conferences. Recife: Joaquim Nabuco Foundation, Edt. Massangana, 2007.

FREYRE, Gilberto. *Casa-Grande e Senzala:* formagao da fam ilia brasileira sob o regime da economia patriarcal. Sao Paulo: Global, 2003.

. *How and why I am and am not a sociologist.* Brasilia: Editora Universidade de Brasilia, 1968.

Interview - Encontros Collection. Organized by Sergio Cohn. Rio de Janeiro January: Beco do Azougue, 2010.

GERSTENBERGER, Debora. "Gilberto Freyre: a theoretical of globalization?". *History, Science, Health - Manguinhos.* Rio de Janeiro, Fundagao Oswaldo Cruz. 2014, vol.21, n.1, pp. 111-120.

GOMES, Candido A. *Darcy Ribeiro.* Recife: Massangana Publishing House, 2010.

GONTIJO, Rebeca. "Manoel Bomfim, 'thinker of History' in the First Republic". *Revista Brasileira de Historia.* Sao Paulo, vol. 23, n° 45, pp. 129-154, 2003.

GOTT, Richard. *Cuba:* a new history. Rio de Janeiro: Jorge Zahar 2006.

IANNI, Octavio. *The Latin American labyrinth.* Petropolis: Vozes, 1993.

JULIO, Silvio. *Bolivar's brain and heart.* Bahia: Livraria progresso Editora, 1957.

LARRETA, Enrique R.; GIUCCI, Guilherme. *Gilberto Freyre uma biografia cultural:* a formagao de um intelectual brasileiro: 1900-1936. Rio de Janeiro: Civilizagao Brasileira, 2007.

LEITE, Dante M. "Manoel Bomfim: essay on the affirmation of the unprotected classes". In. *O carater nacional brasileiro:* historia de uma ideologia. Sao Paulo: Atica, 1992. pp. 250-255.

LIBANEO, Joao B. *The Art of Formation.* Sao Paulo: Loyola, 2002.

LUCA, Tania R. de. The Magazine of Brazil (1916-1925) in the History of the Press. *Travessia.* Revista de Literatura, UFSC, Ilha de Santa Catarina, jan.-jul., pp. 94-123, 1996.

Leituras, projetos e (re)revista(s) do Brasil. Sao Paulo: Edt. UNESP, 2012.

MALATIAN, Teresa M. "Metafora e Nagao: a identidade Latino-Americana em Manoel Bomfim". In: DAYREL, E. G.; IOKOI, Z. M. G. (eds). *Contemporary Latin America:* challenges and perspectives. Collection - America: Roots and Trajectories; vol. 4. Rio de Janeiro: Expressao e Cultura; Sao Paulo: Edusp, 1996. pp.113-121.

MARTI, Jose. "Our America". In: ZEA, L. (Compiler). *Fuentes de la cultura Latinoamericana.* Tome I. Mexico: Fondo de Cultura Economica, 1993. P.119-127.

. "Simon Bolivar". In: ZEA, L. (Compiler). *Fuentes de la cultura Latinoamericana.* Tome III. Mexico: Fondo de Cultura Economica, 1993[2] . p.577-589.

MARX, Karl. *The Civil War in France.* Sao Paulo: Boitempo, 2011.

MARX, Karl; ENGELS, Friedrich. *Manifesto of the Communist Party.* Braganga Paulista: Editora Universitaria Sao Francisco, 2005.

MATTOS, Andre L. L. B. de. *Darcy Ribeiro:* a trajectory (1944-1982). Campinas: Doctoral Thesis in Social Sciences, UNICAMP, 2007.

MATURANA, Humberto; VARELA, Francisco. *The tree of knowledge.* Sao Paulo: Palas Athena, 2001.

MIGLIEVICH-RIBEIRO, Adelia M. "Reflexoes sobre a utopia necessaria e a universidade brasileira". In: VILLAR, J. L. & CARTIONI, R. (ORG.). *Dialogues between Anisio and Darcy.* The UnB project and Brazilian education. Brasilia: Verbena, 20122, p. 27-59.

. "The 1964 Coup, Darcy Ribeiro and exile: paths of memory". Round Table "The 1964 Coup and the memory of Brazilian education". IV International Congress of the Nucleus of Studies of the Americas (Nucleas), Aug 25-29, 2014, Uerj campus, Rio de Janeiro (RJ), *paper.*

. "Darcynian anthropology/anthropophagy and the awareness of intellectual colonialism". In: ALMEIDA, J.; MIGLIEVICH-RIBEIRO, A. M.; TOLLER, H. (org.). *Post-Colonial Criticism:* a panorama of contemporary readings. Rio de Janeiro: Faperj/7 Letras, 20132. pp. 119-138.

"Postcolonial Criticism from Darcy Ribeiro: A Rereading of *The Brazilian People". Revista de Estudos Antiutilitaristas e Poscoloniais,* vol. 1, n° 1. 2011. pp. 127-138.

. "Darcy Ribeiro and Walter Mignolo's Post-Western Critique: Notes on Civilizing Processes in the Americas". *Dimensoes,* vol. 29, 2012. pp. 281-308.

. "Darcy Ribeiro and the *Brazil enigma:* an exercise in epistemological decolonization". *Revista Sociedade e Estado,* vol. 26, n° 2, May-Aug. 20112. pp. 2349.

MIGLIEVICH-RIBEIRO, Adelia M. "Intellectuals and Latin American Self-Consciousness: for a critique of Western reason". *Realis.* Journal of Anti-Utilitarian and Post-Colonial Studies. UFPE. Recife (PE), vol. 3, n° 2, pp. 55-73, 2013.

MIGNOLO, Walter D. *Local histories/global projects. Coloniality, subaltern knowledge and liminal thinking.* Belo Horizonte: Edt. UFMG, 2003.

MORAES FILHO, Evaristo de. Ears of *Latin America: evils of origin.* Rio de Janeiro: Topbooks, 1993.

MORIN, Edgar (org.). *The Religion of Knowledge:* the challenge of the 21st century. Rio de Janeiro: Bertrand Brasil, 2010.

. *Introduction to Complex Thinking.* Porto Alegre: Sulina, 2005.

NASCIMENTO, Roberia N. A. A *Complexidade como Matriz de uma Nova Ecologia Cognitiva.* Joao Pessoa: Doctoral Thesis in Education, UFPB, 2007.

NEPOMUCENO, Eric. *Darcy Ribeiro and the questions I never asked.* January 2011. [Available at: seer.bce.unb.br/index.php/participacao/article/download/7711/5941. Accessed on: 20/02/2014, at 23h17]. pp. 57-59.

NEVES, Cleiton R. das. "Discussing identities: Manoel Bomfim and the Latin American identity discourse". *I Research Seminar of the Post-Graduation in History* - UFG/UCG. Goiania (GO), September 2008. [Available at: http://pos.historia.ufg.br/uploads/113/original_15_CleitonNeves_Discutindoldentidade s.pdf. Accessed on: 15/01/2014 - 22h34].

NUNES, Maria T. "Manoel Bomfim: pioneer of a national ideology". In: BOMFIM, M. *O Brasil na America:* caracterizagao da formagao brasileira. Rio de Janeiro: Topbooks, 1997. pp. 13-25.

ORTIZ, Renato. *Brazilian Culture and National Identity.* Sao Paulo: Brasiliense, 1985.

PALLARES-BURKE, Maria L.; BURKE, Peter. *Rethinking the tropics:* an intellectual portrait of Gilberto Freyre. Sao Paulo: UNESP, 2009.

PALLARES-BURKE, Maria Lucia G. *Gilberto Freyre:* a Victorian of the tropics. Sao Paulo: Editora UNESP, 2005.

. "Gilberto Freyre and England: a love story". *Tempo social.* USP - sao Paulo (SP) 1997, vol.9, n.2, pp. 13-38.

PIETRI, Arturo U. *La creacion del Nuevo Mundo.* Mexico: Fondo de Cultura Economica, 1992.

PINHEIRO, Lucas M. *Darcy Ribeiro e a América Latina*: um pensamento em busca da identidade e da autonomia latino-americanas. Franca: Master's dissertation in History, UNESP, 2006.

PORTO-GONQALVES, Carlos W. "Presentation of the Portuguese edition". In: LANDER, Edgardo (Org.) *Coloniality of knowledge,* Eurocentrism and the social sciences. Latin American perspectives. Buenos Aires: CLACSO, 2005.

PUENTES, Roberto V.; NAVIA, Mario V. *Jose Marti.* Sao Paulo: Icone, 2004.

RIBEIRO, Darcy. "Gilberto Freyre: an introduction to Casa-Grande e Senzala". In: __. *Gentilidades.* Porto Alegre: L&PM, 1997[3] pp. 7-89.

. "Latin American culture". In: ZEA, L. (Compiler). *Fuentes de la cultura Latinoamericana.* Tome I. Mexico: Fondo de Cultura Economica, 1993. pp. 99-118.

. "Manoel Bomfim, anthropologist". In: BOMFIM, Manoel. *Latin America:* evils of origin. Rio de Janeiro: Topbooks, 2005. pp. 11-22.

. *Latin America:* the Great Homeland. Rio de Janeiro: Guanabara, 1986.

. *The Americas and Civilization:* Process of Formation and Causes of the Uneven

Development of the American Peoples. Petropolis: Vozes, 1983.

. *Historical and Cultural Configurations of American Peoples.* Rio de Janeiro: Civilizagao Brasileira, 1975.

. *Confessions.* Sao Paulo: Companhia das Letras, 1997.

. *Mestico e que é bom!* Rio de Janeiro: Revan, 1997[2] .

. *The dilemma of Latin America.* Petropolis: Vozes, 19832.

. *The Brazilian People:* the formation and meaning of Brazil. Sao Paulo: Companhia das Letras, 1995.

The Civilizing Process: stages of socio-cultural evolution. Petropolis: Vozes, 1978.

The Brazilians: 1. Theory of Brazil. Petropolis: Vozes, 19902.

. *Testimony.* Sao Paulo: Siciliano, 1990.

RODRIGUEZ, Pedro P. *Marti and the two Americas.* Sao Paulo: Expressao Popular, 2006.

ROMERA JR., Edison. "Social Sciences and Post-Colonial Studies: between criticism and epistemic enrichment". *Simbiotica.* Electronic Journal. UFES. Vitoria (ES), vol. 1, n° 5, 2013. pp. 86-102.

SADER, Emir. *The Cuban Revolution.* Projeto Passo a Frente: Colegao Guerra e Paz; 2. Sao Paulo: Moderna, 1985.

SANTOS, Agnaldo dos; FERRAZ, Isa G. "Darcy Ribeiro". In: PERICAS, L. B.; SECCO, L. (Orgs.). *Interpreters of Brazil:* classics, rebels and renegades. Sao Paulo: Boitempo, 2014.

SANTOS, Baoventura de S. *Nuestra America:* reinventando un paradigma. Casa de las Americas, n° 237, 2004. [Available at: http://www.ces.uc.pt/myces/UserFiles/livros/158_Nuestra%20America-Casa%20de%20las%20Americas.pdf. Accessed on: 04/05/2014]

SANTOS, Lucas M. dos. *Jose Marti and the identity project of Nuestra America:* an analysis of the construction of American identity. Rio de Janeiro, ANPUH, 2010. P. 09. [Available at: http://www.encontro2010.rj.anpuh.org/resources/anais/8/1276735978_ARQUIVO_TrabalhoAnpuh.pdf. Accessed on: 05/05/2014

SARMIENTO, Domingo F. "San Martin y Bolivar". In: ZEA, L. (Compiler). *Fuentes de la cultura Latinoamericana.* Volume II. Mexico: Fondo de Cultura Economica, 1993. pp. 531-553.

SILVA, Claudia V. A. P. "Contribution of Manoel Bomfim to Brazilian Education". *IX National Seminar of Studies and Research "History, Society and Education in Brazil".* UFP. Joao Pessoa (PB), July-August, 2012. Available at: http://www.histedbr.fae.unicamp.br/acer_histedbr/seminario/seminario9/PDFs/1.33.p

df. Accessed on: 03/02/2014 - 17h12].

SOUZA, Jesse de. "Gilberto Freyre e a singularidade cultural brasileira". *Tempo Social,* Revista de Sociologia da USP. Sao Paulo (SP), vol. 12, n° 1,2000. p. 69-100.

TEIXEIRA, Anisio. "Preface. In: FREYRE, G. *Sociologia:* introducao ao estudo dos seus principios - I. Rio de Janeiro: Jose Olympio, 1967. pp. 1-8.

TRETO, Raul E. G. "La integracion de nuestra America". In: DAYREL, E. G.; IOKOI, Z. M. G. (Coords.). *Contemporary Latin America:* challenges and perspectives. Rio de Janeiro: Expressao e Cultura; Sao Paulo: Edusp, 1996. Pp. 43-53.

VAZ E SILVA, Neusa. *Darcy Ribeiro's theory of culture and intercultural philosophy.* Sao Leopoldo: Nova Harmonia, 2009.

VELHO, Gilberto. "Gilberto Freyre: Trajectory and singularity". *Sociologia, Problemas e Praticas.* 2008, n.58, pp. 11-21.

VELOSO, Mariza. *Jose Marti:* modernity and utopia. Revista Sociedade e Estado. Vol. 26, n° 2. May/August, 2011. p. 133-153.

ZEA, Leopoldo (Compiler). *Fuentes de la cultura Latinoamericana.* Tome I. Mexico: Fondo de Cultura Economica, 1993.

. "Prologue. In: (_ Compiler). *Fuentes de la cultura Latinoamericana.* Volume I. Mexico: Fondo de Cultura Economica, 1993. Pp. 7-9.

Ribeiro Coelho (2012), Helena Bomeny (2001), Neusa Vaz e Silva (2009).

Printed by Books on Demand GmbH, Norderstedt / Germany